METAMORPHOSIS

METAMORPHOSIS

TRANSFORMATION OF A YOUNG TOWNIE INTO A MATURE MEDICAL PROFESSIONAL

DR. SHITAL VINAY PATIL

PARTRIDGE

A Penguin Random House Company

To order additional copies of this book, contact
Partridge India
000 800 10062 62
orders.india@partridgepublishing.com

www.partridgepublishing.com/india

To all my fellow human beings.

PREFACE

India is a great country with diverse traditions and culture. Myths and superstitions exist in the population regarding health care and life at large. *Metamorphosis* is one of a series of books meant to dismantle these vices of the society. It is a fiction based on the medical background meant to slowly decipher and unfold the prejudices about the doctor's profession, people involved in this profession, and life in general. Health care is a major concern for a developing country. Incidences like dowry deaths and female foeticides still continue to persist when we are in fact in the twenty-first century. The tag of a developed nation from a developing nation can never be attached to this country unless the people rise above a certain level of understanding. Modernization has reached its core thinking as far as the use of electronic gadgets and travel are concerned, but relationships and family matters have to undergo transformation for us to make progress.

Acknowledgments

I would like to acknowledge all my dear friends, family members, and acquaintances, including my patients, who taught me a lot in my life. People from my profession and otherwise, those who have been a part of my journey since my early school days that my memory permits me to remember, to the present day, have all contributed in some way or the other in the writing of this book. It is they who developed me into the person I am and gave me the strength to write this book. It is not my book; it is about all the people I have known till date.

Special thanks would go indeed to my husband, Dr Vinay Patil. I would not have written this book without the support and encouragement provided by him and my parents: Dr L. S. Patil, my father, and Mrs Nalini Patil, my mother. My schoolgoing daughters, Shruti and Shivani, have been my biggest critics and have helped me improve and edit my work.

Thanks would be a small word for my publishers for their interest in my work, but nonetheless they need special acknowledgment from the bottom of my heart in their contribution in making this book reach you. The Patridge production team, who edited my work have really done a great job before placing this polished work in your hands. I have no words to thank them too. I would be indebted to them forever.

CHAPTER ONE

I am sitting in my balcony, one lazy rainy Sunday afternoon, watching the raindrops kissing everything they come in contact with. I am wondering at how amazing Mother Nature is. The sun through its rays reaches every corner of this planet. The clouds flow gently, bowing to the wishes of the wind. The sky changes its face so many times in a single day. The moon and the stars give it a tranquil look at night. A thought just crosses my mind, each of these—the sun, the wind, the clouds, the moon, and the stars—are so powerful in themselves. They are being worshipped as gods by man for the strength they possess since time immemorial. People know it forever right from the Stone Age that they have no control over them. They have been there for us all along and will remain with us in perpetuity, scattering their unreserved love for all living beings. Oh! How proud I am, a small tiny being, of their presence and my existence, of my association with them from the time I was conceived in my mother's womb. What if they are too proud of themselves? I wonder, lost in thought. Would they work in a synchronized manner? What if they too have big egos like us humans? They may decide to be lazy. Why does the sun not ask, 'Why does it have to be me? Why do I have to keep shining always, day in and day out, either at one place or somewhere else?' I wish every human being on our planet earth is like the sun, distributing his or her love and affection at all times. Wishes will only be wishes unless we put some efforts for them to be true. We give up easily on ourselves and everything else. It will take generations and generations for people to learn their lessons from these wonders of nature.

I wake up from the deep sombre thoughts that I am in to the incessant ringing of the phone. My landline phone is ringing, whose presence I am rarely aware of. I am a slave of the mobile phone, which is resting peacefully on my table. The landline phone is just there along with the Internet connection I require to survive. Whose phone could this be? There are very few people who know this number. I am walking to receive the phone, but there are thoughts, thoughts, and more thoughts. I wish I could get rid of these. How much of my life I waste in thinking? I keep thinking at all times. There are some people who can block their thoughts. I have heard of the old sages living in another era who were masters of their thoughts, their lives, and who could make all their wishes come true. Wishes were not wishes but the truth for them. I am no sage. I am striving to attain a simplistic lifestyle like them and to give power to my words and thoughts. There are some men and women in today's world who desire a flower and it appears before them. This is the real power of a person's words. What is this magic that a human achieves and how? I am on a journey to seek an answer to this.

I pick up the phone, and before I say a sweet hello, I hear a loud, clear voice, 'Is it Shalinii, Shalinii Mallik?'

Our surname that we have here in India is the reflection of our identity. It denotes our religion, caste, and the area to which we belong. We make a declaration in front of the whole world that we do not believe in discrimination between humans. We nevertheless ask a person's surname first. I am shocked to hear that surname being attached to my name. Who could this be? I scan through my memory to identify the voice. It has been a long time since I heard it, but it sounds familiar. It is a person who is not aware of the current status of my marriage. I do not know how to react. My voice isn't with me. I keep hearing a soft 'Hello, hello' and 'Is it Shalinii?'

I finally find my voice back. I reply in a very slow tone, almost like a whisper, 'Yes, it is Shalinii, Shalinii Jadhav,' with an extra stress on the word *Jadhav*, my maiden surname.

There is a distinct surprise in the voice now. 'Are you Dr Shalinii from the 1989 student's batch from HP College?'

I answer mechanically, 'Yes, it is.'

An excited voice asks me, 'Where is Pawan? You both vanished into the air after your internship. We have been searching for you ever since.'

I have not been paying attention as to who the person is on the other side. It is at that moment I get the identity of the man I am talking to. 'Is it Vishal?' I exclaim.

'It took you so long to recognize me. Anyways, I too have had difficulty in placing you. You sound so different, distant, and unfamiliar. By the way, give him the phone please. I am dying to hear his voice.'

Vishal sounds like a long lost girlfriend of Pawan's. I, on my part, do not know what to say. This is Pawan's best friend, and what do I tell him? I do not want to lie; that is something I have never done all my life. I, though, have a strong urge of lying to him just now. I know how desperately he wants to meet Pawan. But I could not have sustained this lie since I myself do not know where Pawan is.

'Vishal, Pawan and I are not together.' This is all I could say. There is a silence, a silence of Vishal's disappointment that is palpable to me even through the phone that I am holding in my hand.

'I know you have a list of why, what, when, ifs, and buts and you want to know where Pawan is. I want you to believe me when I say I have no idea of where Pawan is in this great big world,' I reply after receiving no communication from the other side for nearly two minutes.

Vishal sighs a heavy 'Ooh'. There is silence again. It is a sad moment for Vishal. He took all the pains to search for us. He must have been so happy on finding my phone number, and now I have no whereabouts of the person he wants to talk to. He is quiet; I am not sure whether he is there or not on the other side. I am uncomfortable with these long pauses of his and have no words to cheer him up.

At last, I end up saying, 'Look, Vishal, I have a caller identification facility on my phone. I shall store this mobile number of yours and call you someday, and we can meet up and talk.'

Vishal gains back his composure and voice. I now hear him say clearly, 'Shalinii, I have called you up to inform you about a get together of our college in December. I promise you, like I have promised the others that I shall find Pawan by then. I am meeting you not someday but coming Sunday if you are free.'

'Vishal I am not in Mumbai', I mumble. 'I stay at a place which is three hundred kilometres from Mumbai. Can you come here?'

'I shall see you coming Sunday wherever on earth you are and shall call you on Friday for your address.'

'Call me whenever you decide to meet me. Bye.' I hang up without waiting for his reply.

I go back to the balcony. I lose the temperament of enjoying the rain. It's been so many years since I have split from Pawan. But his memories haunt me every minute. I am fine with the fact that he is not with me. I have no regrets. I go through such emotionally weak moments once in a while. We have spent so many happy times with each other in the past and would have had many more such times if Pawan would have been with me. We have been through life's ups and downs like most human beings, which had not troubled us then as we had each other for support. We were together, and we had a nicely painted future before us. It is a very strange fact of life that whatever it is we want to forget, something or somebody, it just stays with us. Our brain is not a piece of paper from which we can erase whatever we want to with an eraser. The more we take efforts to get away from things, the more we get closer to them. We cannot and should not try to conceal our memories. We have to learn to be with them. Memories are only memories. They are not good or bad or ugly. They are to be cherished and remembered fondly. These are the times we have been through, and those times are never to come back to us. We make them unpleasant by the meanings we attach to them. We make up our own meanings about everything and see things through our perspective. We rarely put ourselves in some other person's position and see things their way.

The phone once again starts ringing. Even before I pick it up, I know whose phone it is. I am sure it is Vishal who has called me back as an afterthought to ask or talk to me about something that seems important to him. I pick up the phone, and without giving him a chance to say hello, I start talking with an authoritative but subdued tone. I want to convince him on one side that all is fine with me and on the other I actually am down in the dumps. I am trying to hide my own disappointment of not being in communication today with the man I loved so much and who was so much a part of my life once upon a time. Was it some other lifetime? I ask myself. Do I not love him even now and all along these days, months, and years?

'Vishal, what is it?'

'Shalinii, can you tell me when have you last met or talked to Pawan, and where was he at the time you heard about him from anybody? Do you have the slightest idea of where he could be today?'

'Vishal, I do not think I can answer all your questions at once.'

'Shalinii, tell me as much as you know about him, and tell me about the most recent times.'

'Vishal, I have not talked to him in years. I do not remember the last time I met him or heard from him. Maybe it was ten years back. I do not know. Frankly speaking, I do not even know whether he is even alive.'

This is the last straw that hurt Vishal a lot. His voice is deep with emotions, and I can sense it through his muteness that he is fighting the tears welling up in his eyes.

'How can you even say that, Shalinii?' There is a distinct tremble in his voice. 'It is good for him he is not with you today.'

'Do you know what I have gone through all these years?' I retort back.

'I do not care about you and the so-called sufferings you are going through. You have been a crybaby. You cry at the drop of a hat. Is that my friend's fault?'

'I am not talking to you about faults and mistakes in life. My falling in love with Pawan has been the biggest mistake of my life. I request you not to disturb me and my peaceful world. I have put in a lot of efforts to create it after your friend left me halfway. I do not want to answer any of your questions. I am not bound to tell you anything about me or him. Please do not call me ever again.' I emphasize and slam the phone back into its receiver. This conversation has been too much for me to bear, and I break down into a sob. I am crying slowly at first and then uncontrollably for quite some time.

I do not know how long I have been lying on the bed, crying with the pillow over my head. Vishal's words keep coming back to me. He has called me a crybaby. Am I really a crybaby? Am I worthy of the treatment Pawan has meted out to me? Do I deserve being away from Pawan? How did we commit this blunder? Is it we, me or him. I have given my best to our relationship. Where exactly did I go wrong? I do not think I am responsible for our break-up. These and many other thoughts keep creeping up in my brain for a long time. I am pondering over the past. I have no control over what has already happened. I cannot go into the past and change it the way I want it to be. I have been a slave of my circumstances then and am being a slave of the circumstances even today. My life has not moved forward an inch since that day, the day I so well remember, the day Pawan told me he is in love with somebody else and wants a divorce. My world shattered into many pieces then, and it is still that way till today. 'I have moved ahead in life' is what I have managed to convince everybody around me, including myself. I have succeeded a lot professionally. I am doing what I dreamt of since childhood. I have fame, wealth, friends, family, relatives, and a lot of near and dear ones but Pawan.

I have been crying today after a long time, maybe years. I have accepted my life the way it is and taken things in my stride long ago. It is as if I have had a wound which I thought had healed completely, but a small scratch by Vishal and it is bleeding as fresh as if I have got it just yesterday. The Shalinii that Vishal knows of has indeed been undeveloped. People mature with time and age. I too have learnt the lessons of life and grown up. It is my misinterpretation of Vishal's concern for Pawan today which upset me. Maybe I am more distressed with myself. I have not looked back. I have never tried to seek out for Pawan all these years. We could have been friends, the way we were before we got married. It has been my analysis that he left me, ditched me, and has not bothered to think about me or find me.

We interpret people and situations according to our convenience, the way we feel things are. Something that we construe as wrong maybe right for somebody else. But in our righteousness, we make the other person wrong. We think we are right and the other person is wrong. In order to prove how truthful we are, we go to any extent never realizing at what cost we are proving ourselves to be correct. I realize my foolishness. I have not exchanged any pleasantries with Vishal. He has been a good friend of mine too.

I get Vishal's phone number from the received phone calls list on my phone. I save his number carefully in my mobile phone and call him up. He does not have my mobile number. He does not pick up my call at the first instance. I keep repeating the call every few seconds. Finally, I hear an irritated 'Hello' from him.

'Vishal, I am sorry for my behaviour earlier. I want to meet you and talk to you. How are you, and would you like to see me as planned earlier on this Sunday? You can be at my place for lunch. I am sending you my address.' I say all this in one go without even pausing to take a breath lest he disconnects the line.

'Shalinii, I too should not have been harsh on you. I can very well understand your state of mind. We will search for Pawan together. Don't ever say you do not care, I know you care too much. You can fool the whole world, not me. I have seen you both together, and I know the kind of relationship that the two of you share. I shall be at your house Sunday by 11 a.m. Bye.'

Vishal's reassuring words make me feel much better. I message him my residential address. I call up my mother and talk to her every day. It is time to call her up. I go through the routine chores of the day: eating, cleaning, planning for the whole of next week, preparing for work the next day, and praying to God, before going to sleep. It is a regular, usual day, and things are back to normal for me in no time. The day ends before I realize it.

I am in my bed. I am far from sleep. My mother has been a devotee of the Hindu Lord Shiva. She has taught me to chant the mantra of this god during my early childhood days. She has trained me to chant the tune, counting it to an auspicious number on the fingers of my hand. It has become a daily routine for me to chant 'Om Namah Shivay' every day 108 times before I go off to sleep. The magic of this hymn has worked on me to induce sleep many times. I finish chanting 108 times as usual with no results. Sleep has become my adversary today. I have a full working day tomorrow with ten to twelve hours of scheduled work which cannot be postponed unless I fall sick or meet with a major accident. I need a good night's sleep for a nice fresh start of the week. I toss and turn in bed. At last I sit up and turn to my favourite hobby. I start listening to old Hindi movie songs on my mobile's FM radio. There is Kishore Kumar singing one of his naughty songs, and I feel like dancing. I get up and dance to the tunes of the song till it gets over. The next is a sad song by Lata Mangeshkar. I usually like listening to sad songs. Today I am in no mood for it. I give up trying to sleep and do what I actually want to do. I go down memory lane.

CHAPTER TWO

I have passed my twelfth-standard exam with flying colours. I have scored 97 per cent marks in physics, chemistry, and biology, the subject marks required for an admission into a medical college. It has been my dream and a vision of my family for me since childhood that I pursue medicine as a career. My grandfather's grandfather had been the civil surgeon of a district hospital during the British era. Nobody from my family did medicine thereafter. I am at the threshold of fulfilling that dream. I am definitely getting an admission into a medical college. We have higher secondary boards, and we are to take admission according to our merit in the medical college that falls within the domain of our board. I am to pursue the MBBS course which means a Bachelor Of Medicine and Bachelor Of Surgery.

I belong to the holy city of Nashik. The higher secondary board for Nashik is Poona. I am very fond of this city of Pune as it is called. I have spent a few school years here, and I like this city very much. My father gets the Pune medical college admission form. I tell all my friends about me living henceforth in Pune. 'I would visit you during my vacations,' I promise them. My father completes the process of filling up the form and attaching all the necessary certificates. I require my birth certificate, my nationality and bona fide certificates, a blood group report, the academic certificates such as the mark list and passing certificate duly attested. My sports certificates which include my state level certificates in the sports of badminton and basketball would give me extra credit. I bring forth my Bharatanatyam dance certificates to be put in with the rest of the papers. My father informs me that they carry no additional benefit like the sports credentials. My admission form is submitted in the medical college in Pune, and I am eagerly awaiting the interview letter to come to me.

The very next day, I see my father filling one more admission form with all the certificates. I am puzzled, and I ask my father about it. Mumbai, the great capital of the state of Maharashtra, has five medical colleges, and they have 15 per cent all Maharashtra seats, reserved for students from other boards. My father's friend has been to Mumbai to get an admission form to these colleges for his son, and he brought one extra form for me. I have heard and read a lot about Mumbai on the television and the newspaper.

'It is a dangerous city, I am not going there,' I tell my father.

'We are sending the form which does not mean you have to go to Mumbai. You can decide for yourself where you want to go later on,' comes my father's reply.

I receive a letter after a few days and am overjoyed to see it. It is the very first letter I have received in my name. I open it enthusiastically to be disappointed as it is not the letter I have been waiting for. It is the letter from Mumbai, asking me to attend an interview on the 13th of July at HP Medical College. I receive this letter on the 10th of July. The next two days, I am busy packing reluctantly for my journey to Mumbai with my father. The interview is at eight in the morning. We have no close relatives staying in Mumbai.

We decide to go to Mumbai the evening prior to the day of the interview by train. My father makes all the necessary arrangements, advance bookings, and the train ticket. On the day I am to travel, I receive the interview letter from Pune. The interview there is scheduled on the14th of July at 3 p.m. I do not want to go to Mumbai. My father insists that we go to Mumbai first and then to Pune from there.

The time of my departure arrives. I say goodbye to my mother and younger sister, Swaroopa. We board the train, and as the train starts moving, I am apprehensive with the thought of staying in a hostel minus my family. It's the rainy season, and it is raining heavily since morning. The train, in spite of being a fast train, is moving very slowly. It is dark outside even at five in the evening due to the clouds. There is a very strong wind howling outside the compartment. Mumbai's climatic conditions being warm and humid, I have not taken any warm clothing with me. I just have one woollen shawl with me which my mother has forcibly put in my bag. People in the compartment close the windows to prevent rainwater from coming inside. The whole compartment is wet as it is not completely waterproof. I am travelling in the second-class compartment of the Indian railways, shivering and cold. I have never travelled in such a bad weather before. As time passes by, I feel suffocated with the closed doors and windows of the compartment. In my excitement of travelling to Mumbai and then to Pune, I have hardly eaten anything for lunch. The snacks my mother had packed for me have been eaten as soon as I entered the train.

After around two hours of travelling, the train stops. There is no station in sight. The rainfall becomes heavier. It is now difficult to see anything through the glass window.

I have my shawl tightly wrapped around myself and am trying to sleep on my father's lap. More than three hours have passed since we are in this no man's land. We should have been in Mumbai by this time. The darkness around us is increasing and so is the water level. It is midnight, and we do not know where we are. By now, I am hungry. The train moves a few yards, giving all of us a ray of hope. It stops again. I wonder if I would be alive by the time this ordeal is over. As I am watching out through the glass window, there is a flash of lightening enabling me to see in the darkness outside the compartment. The train is surrounded on all sides by water, on the tracks and beyond, which makes me feel as if we are in the middle of a sea. Children in the compartment are alternately crying with hunger or going off to sleep after being tired of crying, and they would all take turns to cry. The train compartment is full of chaos, and there is worry written on everybody's face. Will we ever reach our destination? I sleep more out of fear than drowsiness.

Presently, I am being woken up by my father. The train has moved ahead and it stops at a station where we get off. 'Have we arrived?' I ask my father. 'The train is not moving ahead from here, so we have to take a local train hereafter,' answers my father. It is 5.30 a.m. and still dark outside. There is a gusty wind, but the rain is not heavy, only a drizzle. We get into a local train which leaves us far from where we have to go. We go out of the station onto the road outside. It is day; the ghastly night has ended. The after-effects of the storm are clearly visible to us. Trees have fallen down, blocking the roads at places. Hoardings and boards of shops are lying on the streets. The busy roads of

Mumbai are deserted. My father is desperate to take me for the interview on time and tries to hire a taxi. No taxi man wants to start business. We walk for some time to find a kind soul whom my father convinces that a future doctor in the making would lose the opportunity if we do not reach on time. The taxi driver reluctantly takes us and drops us at the HP College sharp at 9a.m., having changed lanes and by lanes several times to avoid hurdles.

We rush to the office without even having freshened up, to be told that due to heavy rains and a cyclone-like situation the previous night, the interview has been postponed to 14th of July, 8 a.m. I have both interviews on the same day, one in Mumbai in the morning and the other in Pune in the afternoon. I do not know what destiny has in store for me. My father is optimistic. He says we will attend both the interviews. I want us to go to Pune as planned earlier and forget Mumbai. My father thinks otherwise, and we stay. We take a room in one of the nearby hotels and clean ourselves up. After a heavy breakfast, both of us go off to sleep. We wake up in the evening, and on my insistence, my father takes me to Marine Drive to see the sea. It is my first rendezvous with the sea, and I fall in love with it instantly. We spend an hour there. The next day being a big day for me, we go to bed early after a light dinner.

We are at the HP College office at 7.45 a.m. on 14th of July. We are seated in a large hall where students along with their parents are waiting. There is a list of students, as per their merit, displayed on a board. I am among the first ten students as I get additional five marks for my achievements in sports, which takes my tally of marks to 98.67 per cent. Ten of us, parents excluded, are taken to another room before each one of us goes in front of the deans of the five medical colleges. I do not notice fellow students around me. I have a panic attack. What will they ask me in the interview? Should I tell them straight away I do not want to come to Mumbai? Will I be able to answer the questions they ask me? Will I fail the interview? All the students are talking to each other. I think they must be all from Mumbai and must have been friends since school or junior college. We have one junior college in Nashik. If there would have been a medical college in Nashik, I would have had friends with me. I scan every person around me and watch their happy faces chit-chatting with each other. Where am I? Will I be able to identify with these people and belong to this city? I suddenly notice two piercing eyes watching me enthusiastically. Before I ponder over those eyes, to see who they belong to, the girl sitting next to me asks me my name.

'I am Shalinii,' I tell her.

She says, 'I am Paulomy Kulkarni from Ghatkopar.' We shake hands which gives me a feeling of warmth.

'Where and how far is Ghatkopar?' I ask her.

'Oh! It's a suburb of Mumbai that means it is a part of Mumbai. Where are you from? Are you new to Mumbai?'

'I am from Nashik, been to Mumbai three to four times during my childhood for a day or two.'

'Are you two from the same junior college?' I ask her pointing at the girl standing after her whom she has been busy talking to before me.

'You mean Shreya, no, we just met. She is from Thane. Thane is also like a suburb of Mumbai,' she adds, realizing how naive I am.

The interview begins. Two students go in and come out in ten minutes, and then the next two go in. Two more and it is my turn. I start perspiring and am very anxious, when I hear a voice saying, 'Don't worry, the interview is just a formality. They do not ask you any academic questions, relax.' I look up to find the owner of those eyes that I have seen some time ago, addressing me in a gentle sympathetic tone. He has been the first one to go for the interview. I look at him and give him a nervous smile.

I go into the dean's chamber, and the dean of HP Medical College says, 'Why are you in such a hurry to get into a medical college, young lady? We do not admit students into medical school before the age of seventeen, and you are sixteen now. You will have to come next year. We will reserve your seat for the coming academic year. What is your college preference?' I involuntarily say 'HP College', remembering Sunil uncle, my father's friend and my paediatrician. He had said if you are getting admission to HP college, take it, don't refuse.

'Oh! You want to come to my college, fill in the form again next year, and you are welcome to join us, you will be first on the list whatever the merit of that year is. Goodbye.' It is the end of my interview, and I walk out. I go to the clerk sitting in the next room who hands me a letter which says 'Admitted to HP Medical College, seat reserved for next year since underage'.

I see piercing eyes waiting outside the dean's chamber. 'Which college have you chosen?' he asks as soon as he sees me. I reply curtly, 'HP'.

'Good, you are in my class.'

'Not this year, next year.'

'What do you mean by that? You have come here for an advance booking. Have you not passed your twelfth-standard board exam?'

I am laughing for the first time in Mumbai seeing the confused look on his face. 'I am underage for medical education,' I say.

'What is that? I never heard age has anything to do with medical studies. You do not look like a kid to me.' He laughs loudly at his own joke, and by now, we have an audience. Eight to ten students who have finished the dean's visit either before or after me are keenly listening to our conversation.

'I am only sixteen—'

'I am not asking you your age,' he cut me mid sentence. 'I asked you what is underage.'

'I am explaining exactly that, but you are not letting me speak. You seem to me as an impatient boy. The age required to seek admission to a medical college in India is seventeen and I am not seventeen, so I come here next year.' I address the small crowd gathered around us, ignoring Mr Piercing Eyes. I rush to my father as I remember I have to go to Pune, immediately suppressing my wish to tell this recently met group that I am not coming back here ever again as I am going to study at Pune Medical College. I also want to say a very good bye to Mr Piercing Eyes. He would forget this talk by next year, so there is no point. I walk with my father out of the HP College campus, viewing it one last time as if to say goodbye. I like the place and its people.

CHAPTER THREE

It is 9 a.m. My father has been correct; we can attend both interviews with ease. The sky is clear with few clouds. I am happy to take a bus ride from Mumbai to Pune. I enjoy the journey very much. There is greenery everywhere; the sun is bright. The atmosphere is pleasant, neither hot nor very cold. We cross Lonavala; there are clouds there and a mild shower which brightens me up. I see a rainbow through the bus window, and I giggle aloud like a child. I am humming and singing my favourite Kishore Kumar songs all along the way.

We reach Pune hospital and medical college by 1.30 p.m. We have our lunch and reach the auditorium of the college by 2.45 p.m. I have had a reversal of my role and am confident and cheerful. I do not appear to be lost. I observe in detail the room and the people in it. It is a nicely decorated room with carvings from the epic *Ramayana*. It has paintings of various political leaders hung on its high walls. There are groups of students talking to each other. I go to one of the girls standing alone and talk to her. She does not want to interact with me and is waiting for a school friend of hers to come along. My efforts to intermingle with a few other students are met with an obvious disdain. I have to come here next year, not this, and the batch of students then would be better than this, I persuade myself. The interview ordeal gets repeated here, and we are done with my medical college admission by the end of the day.

The experience of the past two days has left me in a baffled state of mind. I feel as if the city of Mumbai has been warning me: Beware, this is how I am, unpredictable. My people are warm, supportive, and accommodative, but I may not always be cooperative. The city of Mumbai never sleeps, and the life here is too fast. You can make your life here or break it. You get what you want, and you ask for more and more. Pune gave me an impression of a well-organized, decorated, and adorned city. The people of this city seem distant and self-centred. Life is at a slow pace. You are self-content and satisfied with what you have in this city. One is willing to absorb anything within its culture, and the other does not want to look further than its own culture. Both are fine cities at the peak of their growth and youth. The choice is going to be mine. I have a year to decide where I seek my fortune. 'Will I be fortunate enough to survive any of these two great cities?' is the question I want to find an answer to, in the coming year.

I come home to my family, friends, and relatives to receive a hero's welcome. What will I do for one whole year? I get free advice from people around me. Do some one-year diploma course. Learn computers; you should be computer literate these days. Why don't you buy medical books and start studying medicine right away? Some people say, 'You should have manipulated your age.' I wonder, if I manipulate something as basic as my date of birth, at the beginning of my career, what kind of a doctor I would turn out to be. Manipulation would be in my blood. My parents have taught me honesty and truthfulness.

My father takes a decision that I should learn whatever I want to without getting admitted to any formal course or the burden of giving exams. I have a year-long vacation to do whatever I want to, with no responsibility before I take the final plunge into a medical career. I have heard stories of how difficult medical education is, and that there are big, large, huge books to read and learn. I do not want to see these books lest I get disheartened and give up the idea of becoming a doctor. I have been a first ranker in whatever I did academically or in sports. Failure is something I will not be able to digest. The fear of failure though lurks high on my mind at all times.

Our actions are limited by this fear of failure. We do not dare to do things we know we can do. How many times do we actually fail in life? Our existence and our lives are rarely threatened. We do not live our lives fully due to fear. We are so intellectually evolved that our brain gives us warning signals without even thinking or evaluating the situation. We give in to fear at all times, and we die a hundred deaths prematurely because of it. In our school, if we do not do well in some subject then we permanently delete it from our life, out of fear. If we fail to achieve something, we attach a tag—can never do this—forever. The difference between failure and success is to keep trying to do the same thing in different ways and never giving up. We give up easily at the first instance and become martyrs in our own eyes. We carry that martyrdom to our graves. What we need to give up is our fear, our ego, our anger, our righteousness, to which we hold on to all our lives. What we need to pursue is our passion, our career, our health, our relationship, our happiness, which we give up easily. We then blame our circumstances and give up being responsible ourselves. It is easy to censure the conditions or situations so as to be out of our own guilt. Why are we guilty? When we know we could have done better and we have not tried to do so, remorse sets in. We can start and do better at any stage of life. The greatest gift to man is his flexibility in life. We stick to our survival instinct. If we look beyond this survival impulse, life is effortless and uncomplicated.

I do a lot of things during the one year I have in hand. I learn to cook. I watch a lot of TV serials. I teach small children. Teaching has been a passion of mine since childhood, and I love children. I read whatever books I can lay my hands on. I have few resources at my disposal in the town that I live in. Time is at a standstill during this one year. I visit all my friends and relatives as if I am going out of the country never to meet them again. I practice Bharatanatyam and try my hand at singing. I am not a singer. I am fond of the lyrics and know them by heart. I cannot cope with the tunes of the songs. I listen to music and give up trying to sing. I am not an artist and no connoisseur. The only subject where I would get a B or C grade during my school days is drawing and painting. I love artists but cannot be one myself. I start writing poetry and make a collection of my poems in Hindi. I am in a small town with limited access to the modern world. My passion for sports is cut off from here on for the rest of my life.

I learn a lot about medical school. Each year of the medical college consists of three semesters; each semester is of six months. The final exams are after the last semester of each year. So we have first, second and third years of MBBS each for one and a half years. After passing the final MBBS exam there is an internship for one year. The degree of MBBS is complete only after these five and a half years.

We are then eligible to put *Dr* in front of our names. We can go for any postgraduate course either in India or abroad after this, or we can practice as a general practitioner or family physician. In India we have other medical degrees available. Students can opt for the BAMS, which is Bachelor In Ayurvedic medical science, the ancient medicine of India. BHMS is Bachelor In Homeopathy medical science. There are also Unani medical healing techniques. MBBS is the most recent allopathy medical science. Each of these healing processes is great. The allopathy degree is the only one recognized in most other countries. Students often take degree in one medical science in India and practice another, which is ideally not beneficial as far as patients are concerned. Some people with fake medical degrees or who have degrees in nursing also practice medicine. It is not good or bad to treat patients in other forms of medicine than the one in which a person has been educated. It is like a commerce graduate taking history lessons or a literature graduate teaching math. People in India are well educated but are too simple to understand these complexities of the medical system. We Indians are so bound by what has been passed on to us by our previous generations that we are not willing to look at any recent advances.

There is one more problem. The rules, regulations, and instructions of one science are applied and confused with those of the others. This is not just done by the patients but, more often than not, by the practitioners practicing cross-pathies—that is, with a degree in one medical faculty and practicing another. The result is a lot of superstition, myth, and ultimately chaos and confusion among patients. Doctors were worshipped next to God at one time. Today every genuine doctor is looked upon with suspicion. Doctors do not need to be treated equivalent to God. They apply their knowledge and experience to cure the sick. They should at least not be looked upon as criminals. The general consensus about doctors in the population is of mistrust and doubt. There have been quacks, a few greedy doctors, actors and a lot of esteemed people of the society, who have contributed to create this image of the urban doctor. If doctors go on a strike, they are advised to protest in some other way. Who pays attention to the overworked doctors or their odd working hours? When it is a question of the doctor's rights, he becomes superhuman.

Every doctor takes the Hippocratic Oath after the completion of his or her degree. It is a very important promise made to himself, his colleagues, teachers, and patients. We forget the pledge taken every day in school for about ten to twelve years. It is easy for us to overlook the vow taken once in a lifetime. It is high time the oath is modified in keeping with the recent times. The oath was written at a time when the society was free from contemporary evil. Most of us are bound by this oath, and we abide by it. The oath reads as follows.

I, Dr Shalinii Jadhav, solemnly pledge myself to consecrate my life to the service of humanity;

I will give to my teachers the respect and gratitude which is their due;

I will practice my profession with conscience and dignity;

The health of my patient will be my first consideration;

I will respect the secrets which are confided in me;

I will maintain by all the means in my power the honour and noble traditions of the medical profession;

My colleagues will be my brothers;

I will not permit considerations of religion, nationality, race, party politics, or social standing to intervene between my duty and my patients;

I will maintain the utmost respect for human life, from the time of conception; even under threat, I will not use my medical knowledge contrary to the laws of humanity;

I will keep these promises solemnly, freely, and upon honour.

The oath ends here. It demonstrates the nobility of the doctor's profession. There is no other civilian profession so close to humanity, where a person pledges his own life and gives it less importance than the life of a sick person. We give up on ourselves, our families, celebrations, important events, occasions, and festivities for the sake of our patients. We are the perfect example of selflessness and sacrifice. How much does a doctor earn, everyone notices, but at what cost, nobody wants to know. A person who may be suffering from pain in the abdomen since four days decides to go to a doctor since the pain has worsened. He wants the doctor to attend to him immediately irrespective of whether he is celebrating his son's birthday or his brother's wedding or mourning his wife's death or has just been back from his mother's funeral. A doctor is an epitome of humanity and is supposed to be a custodian of all human rights. What about his rights as a human being?

CHAPTER FOUR

A chance glance at the watch shows it to be 5 a.m. It's the time most people wake up, and I have not even slept. I shut down the computer of my brain and bring myself back into the present. Even if I do not sleep, I want to lie down and rest my body and mind. I have to block my thoughts. I start meditating and am asleep in no time. I wake up to the alarm's ringing at 7 a.m. I have had a dream and am not sure of the reality. I have dreamt of the get together and Pawan being present for it. I have no time to think about it right now. It's a Monday, the first day of the week after a holiday, and work is always heavy on Monday. I have to get going in half an hour's time. My OPD—that is the outpatient department—at Mandar hospital starts at 8 a.m. I receive a call from Ruby, the sister in charge of the paediatric department at Mandar hospital to inform me that I have an appointment of 100 patients in both the wings of the hospital, fifty in each wing. Mandar hospital is a charitable hospital managed by two separate trusts. Each wing is handled by a trust belonging to a local politician. It is difficult for me to manage both the wings at times as the interests of the politicians clash with each other. Ruby being in charge of the whole hospital balances things effectively.

I am at the hospital and have finished twenty-five patients when I receive a phone call. 'Shalinii, Vishal here.' He speaks as soon as he realizes I have taken the call, before

I manage to say anything, without the formalities of a 'Hi!' or 'Hello!'

'Pawan is in Chicago, USA. I have not found his address or phone number. I am going through the medical journal of urologists at our college, and I found an article written by him. After I spoke to you yesterday, I decided to come and search the journals. Since I am an alumnus at HP, I can use the library. I came here first thing in the morning and have gone through dozens of journals. I know Pawan cannot live without his academics. I have been lucky.'

'That is good. But how will you find his contact number?'

'I will contact the publishers of this journal. They are bound to have his details. If not, how far is Chicago? I will go there personally and find him and meet him.'

'Tell me if you learn anything about him. Bye.'

The phone line gets cut without a reply. How eager this man is? The commitment he has for Pawan is tremendous. I wish he has the same commitment towards his own life. I have no time to think; Sister Jidha is asking me whether she can send the next patient in, and I nod my head. These Keralite sisters are sincere and systematic. I love working with them. They have a real love for the profession, and they know what nursing care means. It is in their blood. In the Middle Eastern countries, there are so many of these sisters in the medical profession that for the local people, Kerala represents India. The literacy rate of Kerala is also the highest. They have women empowerment there. It is one of the few states in India where, after the marriage of a woman, she retains her maiden name and surname. In the rest of India, a woman attaches the name and surname of her husband, whereas in Kerala, her children are also known by her surname. People of Kerala know to give, and they get back in abundance. They know what it is to be of service to mankind.

I finish examining my patients and rounds of the admitted patients in the wards of both the wings. It is already past 3 p.m. I have a meeting with the urban development council of the town planning department of the municipality at 4 p.m. The municipal corporation is planning a hospital to cater to the people of the neighboring area. They want health facility requirements and inputs from a doctor's point of view. I have been instrumental in getting this project sanctioned, and they expect me to work as an expert on it. Today a member from the health department of India has to survey the feasibility of the project, the budget, and the land allotment for this work. I have to have a separate meeting with the municipality engineers before this final meeting with the sanctioning authority. In less than an hour's time, I have to finish my lunch and be ready with the prerequisites. Ruby rushes in with freshly cut fruits, biscuits and a cup of iced tea for me. She always fills in when I am short of time.

'It's high time you have a personal secretary to take care of you or better still, why don't you get married?' Ruby's question while handing the food to me comes unexpectedly, and I have no answer. I am too preoccupied by the thoughts of the meeting and my presentations. Ruby is about my age and a mother of two lovely schoolgoing daughters.

She treats me like one of her daughters. At such times, she is always quick to add, 'You are a doctor, you know better to take care of yourself, why do you neglect your health?' Ruby seems to be in an unusual frame of mind today. She is not aware of the fact that I have been married once upon a time. 'Did you hear? You can do all this work and have a family. You are young and energetic today, but think of it when you grow old.'

'Ruby, you are now talking exactly like my parents. Can we please discuss this issue some other time? By the way, why is everybody so terrified of old age?' I ask her while sipping tea. Ruby is a bit dispirited, but she is not the one who would give up easily. She continues to tell me the advantages of a happy marriage. I am going through my presentations, and I have Ruby talking to me continuously. I cannot concentrate on anything.

I do not lose my temper often, but my lid has been blown off. I remember similar incidences with my mother so many times that I forget it is Sister Ruby sitting in front of me right now, and I see my mother there.

'I have tried it out once and failed. The memories of that marriage still haunt me. Whenever I sit in front of the mirror, I feel I have been a failure, and I see my husband's face in front of me. Marriages are not always happy one's like you think,' I shout out loud and clear.

Ruby is stunned and does not react for some time. 'I always thought you had something hidden behind that tough exterior and sweet smile of yours. I never thought it would be this,' she says after some time.

I immediately go out of the room towards the washroom to wipe the tears already there in my eyes and to freshen up. I then enter the meeting hall back with my usual stance and poise. Did time turn me into an actor? I wonder. The dummy meeting with the locals and the next one with the government authority go well. Things are materializing the way I want them to, and I am happy. My consultation at Chiranjeev Hospital, which is a private hospital at a place twenty kilometres from where I am, begins at 6 p.m., and I start receiving calls from there while the meeting is going on. I am not in a position to go to see patients as this meeting extends more than its stipulated time, and it has taken my vigour away. So I ask them to keep only the emergency patients for me and cancel the rest of the appointments and transfer them to the next day. The receptionist over there is surprised, and She asks me with concern whether I am fine. I have not taken any holiday other than a few Sundays in the past five years.

The meeting is over at 7.45 p.m. As I walk out, I notice Sister Ruby waiting for me outside the meeting hall. Her duty has finished at 5 p.m. She gets up and walks towards me as soon as she sees me. 'Sister Ruby, why are you here?' I ask her surprised.

'Madam, I just want to say sorry. I did not know anything about your marriage. Whatever I was saying then was out of concern for you. You look after the whole world, and there is nobody to take care of you, I genuinely am worried,' she says affectionately.

'It's fine, sister, I know you love me. You need not have waited for three hours to say sorry. At the most, a phone call would have sufficed. I am not angry with you.' Saying this, I hug her. I can see she is crying, and I wipe her tears. 'It's a long and old story which I shall tell you someday. We loved each other a lot, my husband and me, but it was this love that came in our way and separated us. Do not worry about me, and go to your family, sister. See you tomorrow morning.' So saying, I get out of the corporation building with Ruby. She moves to her parked bike and I to my car.

I go to Chiranjeev Hospital to find that Prashant, a junior colleague, has managed most of the patients. As I am about to leave, Prashant receives a phone call from the neonatal intensive care unit (NICU); a child is gasping there. We run to the NICU together just in time to revive the baby. The baby is going to require an artificial respiratory machine. I start the preparation for that while Prashant goes to explain the condition of the baby to the relatives and to take their consent for artificially ventilating the baby. He comes back with the consent in five minutes, and we put the baby on artificial respiration.

'It's a female child and so the chances of survival are better,' I tell Prashant. Nature has made females better survivors than males right from birth. It is the survival of the fittest even here. I love these small wonders of the world, but it is painful to see them in trouble. The rhythm of the baby's respiration is smooth now. We check all its parameters on the attached monitor, and they are all fine. Prashant adjusts the monitor of this baby on the central small computer screen from where he can monitor the baby continuously. I take a quick round of the other babies in the NICU.

'Whose duty is it at night?' I ask Prashant since it is already 9 p.m., and Prashant's duty ends at 10 p.m.

'It is Shasha tonight,' replies Prashant.

'Ask her to call me up after finishing her rounds to update me regarding all the babies.' Shasha guards the lives of the babies of this ward like a warrior, and I can retire for the day.

I am driving my car at top speed as if trying to get away from somewhere and something. Can a human being get away from her own thoughts? Though I have been rejuvenated and satisfied by saving that baby's life in the NICU, Ruby's questioning face comes up again in front of my eyes. It's the same expression that I have seen so many times on the faces of so many people. I have come far away and settled in this remote place to avoid all the near and dear ones, in search of my own happiness. The shadows of the past still loom high and large on me. There has not been a single day in my life when I have not remembered Pawan. Whenever I am in a fix, I imagine what Pawan would have done in such a situation, and I act accordingly. Sometimes I wonder if I have become schizophrenic. As if I am oscillating in two time zones, one from the past and the other the present, with entirely different characters. I am at present doing what I always wanted to do since childhood. I have been an idealist and a socialite. I derive my strength and my satisfaction from being of service to people. I love being with the people. I am with them when they need me, and I move ahead as soon as my role in their life is over. My life is all about spreading joy and happiness among people. The other life I am living is all about Pawan, love for him, sacrifices for him, and goodwill for him.

I reach home and eat the dinner prepared by Parvati. Parvati is like a family to me. She stays close by and comes every morning to my house to do all the cleaning, washing, and tidying up before she goes to bring her eight-year-old from school. She cooks dinner in the evening. We meet each other mostly on Sundays. She wants to prepare breakfast for me, but that is the time she has to leave her tiny one at school, so I do not allow her. I first met Parvati at a rehabilitation camp in a nearby village. She had come there along with her husband and four-year-old son. Her neighbour brought her and told me that both husband and wife work at a construction site and are addicted to alcohol. They spend whatever they earn in drinking alcohol. They fight over petty matters and neglect their child. We are a team of doctors at the camp. I explain to them that I am a paediatrician, and I am here to look at juvenile addicts. Parvati is desperate to give up her addiction for the sake of her child. She wants me to see them since it is her child who is suffering. I manage to enrol them with a psychiatrist on my team for de-addiction. Both husband and wife are unclean, unhygienic, and underweight, and the child is malnourished.

One day they walk in my OPD after a year for the child's vaccination. Parvati touches my feet no sooner than she walks in. It is customary in India to touch the feet of an elder or respectful person. It is a way of expressing love and respect. I do not recognize them. They are now clean and healthy. Parvati tells me how the treatment has been of value to them. She thanks me for helping them. I tell her that I have done nothing. It is their resolve to get out of the horrible situation they are in that mattered most. They are driven by their own welfare and are gaining from the de-addiction centre we have started. Her husband works as a driver with the contractor with whom they were working as labourers, and their son goes to a government school. It is she who insists that she would manage all my household work. When I refuse her, Parvati feels it is because they are from a lower caste. I have to relent to her request. I do not agree to the caste system, prevailing in India.

I sleep immediately after dinner, which is not good for health. I am too tired to do anything else. I wake up to the sound of heavy rain, thunder, and lightning. It is dark yet. It's almost like a rainstorm outside. I have been petrified of storms since childhood. I love rain, but the associated thunder and lightning are a big no for me. It is akin to liking a person for his qualities and disliking certain things about him, some part of his total personality, some habit of his or someone associated with him. When you choose a person to be your friend or spouse, it is a complete package, a complete human being in totality. These are the only relationships that you can choose. In all other blood relationships inclusive of your parents, siblings, and relatives, you have no choice. You have to choose them anyways. The more you resist your family, the more your life becomes a burden for you. Nobody is perfect, and when you hear the word compromise, it sounds so discouraging. Life is not a compromise. When you accept things the way they are along with all the good and the bad, it is not a compromise. You are happily accepting the situation the way it is or a person the way he or she is, with no misgivings. That is the essence of a human being.

I remember a similar storm I have witnessed in the fourth year of my stay in Mumbai after having joined HP Medical College. It is a storm I will never forget. I am offended because of the storm outside and distressed as a result of the storm inside my head. This is the day Pawan has proposed marriage to me. I am only twenty years old. I am not sure of anything in my life, I have my third year exams approaching and to top it all, there is this—Pawan's proposal. I am in a pathetic state of mind. I am not ready for any commitment, and Pawan wants a lifetime commitment. I do not know why he chose this particular time. I cannot give him any commitment. My career is important to me.

After being in complete hibernation for one year before joining a medical college, I have only studies on my mind until the time I become a medical graduate. Every other thing is like a waste of time for me.

It is dawn. Though the storm subsides in sometime, heavy rainfall continues. It is not rare to have this kind of rainfall in this part of Maharashtra state. I am in a small town Dhadgaon in Nandurbar District. It is a hilly terrain with the local tribal people staying in small groups. Survival of people here is tough. Illiteracy and poverty prevail more than anyplace else. I have been staying here and fighting all odds since ten years. I have seen this town built in front of my eyes. A town did not exist here previously. People stayed in scattered hamlets all over the place. I have come here with simply a desire—desire to give, desire to build, and desire to initiate this town. I am an ordinary person. I do not have the kind of money that builds empires. I have the courage, the willingness, and the eagerness to go on and on and on, no matter what life throws at me. I am like a vagabond, like a wanderer who has nothing of his own. I have nothing to lose or gain in life. The whole world is my family, and I belong to everyone and everyplace I go.

The sky is unusually loaded with clouds. I switch on the TV to realize the lack of electricity. I put on the local station on my battery-operated radio. There is a forecast of very heavy to moderately heavy rainfall in the whole town for the next twenty-four hours. People are being advised to stay indoors. I am experiencing this situation for the first time since I have been to this place. I receive a phone call from Mandar hospital informing me that the outpatient department will remain shut today and that I should not venture out of the house for the day. I call up the municipal town house for the availability of food stores. The local people stay in small hamlets and huts which would not survive this rain. Provisions are made in the municipal town house which is a three-storied building for such times. There are certain places where no vehicle reaches and people have to walk down a few kilometres. The news stated that extra vans have been deployed to transfer people to safety. The regular means of transport are vans and jeeps which can survive this rough ground. Electricity would be out for two to three days. My inverter battery will not survive that long. I search for candles and diyas for light at night. I have no work to do, and I open my cupboard locker to go through the diary I have written after entering medical college. I have not dared to read it from the time I wrote it. I have tried to disregard everything related to Pawan. I left Mumbai and did not keep in touch with any of my old friends.

When a person loses something very dear to him or her, the mind initiates a complex compensatory mechanism. We start hating all that matters to us the most. We tend to dissociate ourselves from people and in turn become isolated. We create entire new worlds. We are at competition with ourselves to prove that what we have is better than what we lost. Things, places, people are there, but they cease to exist for us. We label them as mine, hers, or his. Why can we merely not be with what we think we lost and deal with it graciously and with a big heart? The language of the universe is straightforward: give whatever is possible, take whatever you get back, both with open arms and mind. Dance to the tune of life; go with the flow. Do not measure or calculate what you get and what you give. The question troubling me is, why me? Why do I have to suffer? I do not deserve this. We are no one to decide who is worthy of what. The next question would be then who decides? The answer by 80 per cent God-fearing people would be God, the supreme power. Where is God? God resides in each one of us. We created God for our advantage. We need somebody to transfer the blame on. God and destiny are easy to hold responsible. We are experts at shrugging off responsibility. Why? It is merely for the feel-good factor. We are bent on making ourselves feel good at any cost. Human beings are the most selfish and self-centred animals on earth. The minute we dismantle the feel-good factor, life is beautiful. We should be able to create the feeling of goodness ourselves on the spur of a moment. We are capable of doing it. We instead like to pity ourselves. We love self-pity which is worse than committing suicide. We are excellent at punishing ourselves. Punishment cannot undo damages already made. We want to conquer the world on our terms and conditions. Nothing exists for us than our own disintegrated self. We are blind to the beauty around us. The magnificent nature surrounding us is a spectacle. There is splendor in a child's laughter. We do not marvel at our uniqueness. I have not seen any two exactly similar human beings on this planet. We have the light of life and we long for darkness? There cannot be bigger fools than us. We are happy being fools than being responsible. One fine day, we cease to exist, and all that is important to us goes down into the dirt with us. The truth is we are born and we die one day. The quality of life we live for ourselves and our surroundings is the substance of our life. Nothing else matters.

CHAPTER FIVE

I get ready to be admitted to HP College after lot of persuading from the elders in my house. 'Education in Mumbai is first class,' my mother says.

'I might fall in bad company and start taking drugs,' I argue. 'I am not familiar with the city nor do I have anybody there to take care of me.' I raise another doubt.

'You will have better exposure to patients and the postgraduate seats are more,' my father tells me.

'People do not get a chance to be educated in that great city, you have got the opportunity. You should make the most of it.' This is Sunil uncle who loves me as much as his own daughter. My family and extended family of friends and relatives talk me into going to Mumbai.

I enter the college premises, and as I am walking towards the office, I see Mr. Piercing Eyes waiting there. 'So you are here. I knew you would come. I saw your name the day the admission list was put up,' he says.

'Can you please tell me your name before we talk about anything else?' I ask him. I am referring to him as of now as Piercing Eyes, which I find awkward.

'You forgot my name, Shalinii?'

'No. I have a good memory, and I am proud of it. You never told me your name.'

'You didn't ask.'

'So now tell me your name.'

'Can you guess?'

'How can I guess your name? What is the probability of one guessing another person's name? It may not be possible even after a hundred guesses.'

'Just give it a try, you might be right.'

I think this man is crazy. I want to get going with other things, and so I just say, 'Is it Sagar, Pawan, or Badal?' I am fond of nature, and these represent the sea, the wind, and the clouds in the local language.

'Don't you watch some Hindi movies? I am in most of them. I am Raj.' This is the commonest name in Hindi movies.

'Hi! Raj, I am happy to see you. I have to go to pay my fees and complete the admission formalities. I shall see you later.' Saying this, I stride towards the office. I do not want to have any male associations at present, I tell myself.

I stand in the queue for the fees. It is here that I meet Sushant, Anil, Mandar, Aarti, Saroj, and Prachi. We are told to proceed to the anatomy department after we finish paying the fees. On reaching there, we are asked to come in groups of four. Aarti, Prachi, Saroj and I form one group and enrol ourselves. We are to be each other's dissection partners henceforth. We realize there is nothing for us for the day, and disperse. We have the dean's address to the newer recruits in this seemingly military camp the following day sharp at 9 a.m. in the main lecture theatre, which is called the MLT in short.

I go to the ladies hostel to stay. It is a spacious building with a big corridor in the centre and rooms on all the sides of it. There is a lawn in front of the building. A mess or a dining hall, a visitor's room, and a TV room on the ground floor.

There is a small study room in the centre of all the other rooms. A staircase leads to the girls' rooms. It is a seven-storied building with thirty rooms on each floor. I am told that nobody other than the girls staying in the hostel have the permission to take the stairs and go on the higher floors. Any visitor, male or female, can be on the ground floor only. The mess hall serves tea, breakfast, and dinner on all days except Sundays when dinner is off the menu. The food is at a subsidized rate, and breakfast costs us only one rupee per day. I am too scared of being ragged, having heard so many stories about ragging in colleges and hostels. Our immediate seniors have their first MBBS exam term going on, and they have no time for us. I am the only one staying in the hostel with a senior friend since the official hostel allotment is a few days away. My father leaves for Nashik on the day of the admission itself. I am left alone in a big unknown city to manage myself and my career.

I eat the food packed by my mother for the journey that first day since I am afraid to move out of the room. I am a small townie not out of its cocoon to face the world outside. At night my roommate, Ruchi, goes to a friend's room to study, and I am alone in the room trying to sleep. I take time to sleep in a new place. I hear somebody enter the room and put on the light. I pretend to be sleeping.

'Shalinii, wake up, I am Pooja from second year.' I hear a melodious voice calling me. I open my eyes and sit up.

'Why did you not have your dinner in the mess hall? How can you starve? We do not allow anybody to go without food in our hostel,' she continues.

'I am not hungry,' I say in a tone asking her to shut up and walk away.

'It is an order that you eat food just now, or we will not allow you to sleep tonight.' She says it in a way that I know she will actually do what she says. I go with her to the mess hall.

'I am also from Nashik, and I know how you are feeling. This college is like a school, and you will be protected all along.' I am surprised she already knows where I come from.

I have an uneventful, tasteless dinner. I am not used to eating outside food. My face shrinks as I remember my mother and the delicious food she cooks for me. I have been fussy about food, and she has had to prepare special dishes for me every once in a while. I see Pooja eyeing me, and I try to gulp the food with sips of water after each morsel. 'You will slowly get used to the food,' she says aloud.

As we are climbing the stairs to reach my room on the second floor, I hear somebody whisper 'Grand joon already here.' My pulse quickens as I see a group of seven to eight girls talking in the corridor of the second floor. I prepare to dart into my room.

A third-year student Tanvi says, 'Pooja, we want to talk to your friend.'

I am at my wits' end and at a loss as to what to do. I want to disappear, but my legs become feeble. I stand still as I hear Pooja say 'She is all yours' as she goes into her room next to the stairs. I feel betrayed. I have developed a liking for Pooja. She is caring, and I am annoyed as she walks off, leaving me an innocent prey in front of this hungry pack of wolves. I make up a brave face and look at the floor. To my surprise, I hear a tender person ask me my name, and I look up to see who it is. They are all third-year students, and they tell me ragging is a way of introduction. They acquaint me with their names and the places they have come from. This hostel has girls who have come from outside the limits of the municipal corporation of Mumbai. Soon I become a part of the group. They give me information regarding the rules of the hostel, the food in the mess, the various canteens, and day-to-day functioning of the college. I am at ease with them. There is no making fun of me, no troubling me, or making me do odd tasks. I pinch myself and realize I am not dreaming as I feel the pain. It is the beginning of the shattering of the myths that I am carrying about this college, this city, and this place called the ladies hostel of HP College. I sleep a sound sleep for the first time in an unknown place with compassionate girls around me. I dream of being at home with a new family of girls.

I open my eyes as the alarm that I have set in my table clock starts ringing. I put it off and get out of bed, tiptoeing lest I make a noise and wake up Ruchi who has slept I do not know when. The time is 6 a.m., and I am sure I will not be late on my first day of college. As I proceed to the bathroom with my bucket, I see a big row of buckets one after the other in a queue. There is nobody in sight, and I barely hear the sound of the hot water from the geyser falling in the bucket. I start brushing my teeth, keeping the bucket beside me.

'Queue up your bucket if you want to have a bath with warm water.' I know it's Pooja without looking around as she picks up her bucket full of hot water and goes in one of the four bathrooms for a bath. The geysers are installed two each outside the set of four bathrooms, and there are four sets of such bathrooms on each floor. I learn the first lesson of the hostel life—have a bath at odd times or wake up before 5 a.m. to have a lavish bath.

I reach the college side of the campus, which is about a ten minutes' walk from the hostel, at 8.30 a.m. I do not know where the MLT is. I am on the lookout for it when I get caught by some students sitting near the college entrance.

'Hey! A grand joon!' By now I have become familiar with the word, and there is nobody around so I know the subject of their reference is me. I stop in my tracks and am surrounded by four to five girls and boys in no time.

'Which college are you in?' I am asked. 'Which college were you in previously?' I am bombarded with questions, and I keep looking at them. 'Why have you come to medicine?'

I remember the definition of ragging I have heard the previous night and I screech, 'Will you let me talk so that I can introduce myself?' There is complete silence before I begin to talk. 'My name is Shalinii Jadhav, and I am from DSK Arts, Science, and Commerce College in Nashik. I am right now in HP Medical College.'

'What is the full form of HP?' is the next question. I stare at them blankly as I do not know it.

'Can you see that statue there?' One of them points towards a statue right at the entrance of the college. 'Go and read the name and touch the feet of that statue.'

As I approach the statue, I can read Harkisondas Parshuramdas written on the nameplate at the bottom. I touch the feet of that statue with genuine respect for the man who is the founder member, and the source of the first medical college in India. His calm and serene face makes me appreciate the greatness of the man.

As I turn back, I hear the group whispering, 'Has she fallen in love with the statue? What is she doing?'

'Will you kiss the statue on its lips now?' I am being ordered to do something bizarre. I want to offset the dominion on me. I do not obey their command.

Before I reach the group, Ruchi, my room-mate at the hostel, comes to my rescue. 'What are you doing here, Shalinii? You are supposed to be in the MLT by now. The dean is never late,' she scolds me.

I look at the other students before answering Ruchi. Taking a clue that I would complain to Ruchi about them, they go away, and Ruchi guides me to the MLT.

I enter the grand main lecture theatre, and I am amazed by its grandeur and size. Whenever I have been in this room before, it was not with a sense of belonging. It was out of compulsion, not by preference. It is not the same henceforth. I am now a part of this grand heritage. It has a capacity of 3,000 chairs, and the 200 of us look like few scattered mice on a huge mountain. The dean enters exactly at 9 a.m., and he requests us to rearrange ourselves and sit in the front rows with no gaps in between. We oblige and we are seated in no time. The dean begins his address.

'You are in one of the best and prestigious medical colleges in the whole of the continent of Asia. This college is known for its discipline and excellent education. I am aware that, like every year, we have the cream of Maharashtra here with us today. I know each one of you has scored well in your higher secondary education and have been toppers in your respective colleges. I do not underestimate your capabilities. But medical education requires, along with intelligence, hard work, and sincerity, a lot of perseverance, faith in yourself and others, and love and compassion for the patients. You are going to be with us for five and a half years, and I hope by the end of it, I make you worth serving the people in a gigantic way. The amount of money the government pays for you to have that *Dr* prefixed before your names is too high. I want you to pledge right now that you will be of service to the sick until your last breath. I want you to be conscious of the reputation of this college and not indulge in any kind of antisocial activities during your stay with us. If any of you is not sure about the course in life they want to take, do not waste this medical seat which has been allotted to you. Let the next person in the waiting list move ahead and get an admission if you are sure you do not want to do medicine or have been forcibly sent by your parents or your guardians. Do whatever you want to do but please do not waste your time and our time.

'I welcome you all from the bottom of my heart and wish you the best of luck for your journey at HP Medical College. We have given the best of physicians, surgeons, gynaecologists, and paediatricians to the world, and I am confident we shall not fail in our mission. The Department of Anatomy is on the first floor of this same building, physiology is on the second floor, and biochemistry is on the third floor. These are the three subjects you will be learning this year. Your timetable has been put up outside the anatomy department, and your classes and complete regular functioning starts from tomorrow. Let me introduce you to Dr Mrs Dahale who is the head of the Department of Physiology.'

A short fair lady with a peaceful face climbs on the stage and stands next to the dean. A man with a starched and well-ironed white dress is the next to go on stage.

'This is Dr Jain, and he manages the anatomy department,' says the dean, pointing towards the person who just climbed the stage.

'Miss Deshmukh, please come on stage,' announces the dean, and I see the most beautiful lady in her early thirties going up the stage. There is a clear and loud murmur among the students. She is no less than a Bollywood actress.

'She is the youngest on my team of teachers for you, and she handles and heads the Department of Biochemistry.'

'We are all available in our offices on our respective floors, and you can meet us any time in case you have any problem.' The first to begin talking is Jain sir, and he looks indeed the friendliest of them all.

'You are here to learn a profession, not on an observer post or a tour of this campus. Your conduct should be of utmost accountability, and we do not tolerate irresponsible behaviour,' pitches in Dahale madam, who seems to be the strictest of all. One and all eagerly wait to hear the voice of Deshmukh madam, but she just smiles at all of us.

'The list of your roll numbers has been put on the physiology noticeboard. The sitting arrangement for all the lectures in the lecture halls is according to your roll numbers,' says Dr Mrs Dahale.

'The anatomy dissection begins at 11 a.m., and the first batch begins dissection from tomorrow,' Dr Jain says this.

All our teachers wish us best of luck, and we sing the national anthem together before we scatter.

I make a few friends and start looking for girls who would be with me in the hostel. I find four of them: Ragini from Amravati, and her schoolmate Poorvi, Simran from Delhi who has come from the all India entrance exam, and

Poonam from Aurangabad. I ask my newfound friends to have food with me in the college canteen. They are staying with their relatives in the suburbs of Mumbai. They are not willing to go to the canteen out of the fear of getting ragged. I have become secure by now, and I persuade them to come to the canteen. I have not had any food other than home-cooked before. I am all eager to visit the canteen. In fact, I am on my own for the first time in my life, and I enjoy this newfound freedom of mine very much. There are weaker moments though when I miss my parents and my home.

'Didn't you hear the dean say that no antisocial activities will be allowed on campus and that we could complain if we have any problem?' I tell them. Ragini and Poorvi agree since they have each other and are not fearful. Simran is elder to us by two years, and she is in no doubt.

The only person hesitant is Poonam, but I influence her to come. 'Do not show on your face that you are new here. Pretend to be certain of your steps, and nobody will recognize us,' I warn them.

We reach the canteen to find it overflowing with people, students, professors, with no vacant place to sit. We decide to wait there and find students sharing tables.

We too find a table occupied by two girls and take their permission to share it. 'Grand joons?' they ask us. Two of us nod our heads as yes, and two of us nod as no. They come to know from our nervous faces and their uncertainty turns into reality the moment we ask the waiter for a menu card. The waiter points to the wall behind our backs at the farthest corner. It takes us some time to see the menu written on the wall.

'Why are you in a medical college?' asks one of the girls. All of us reply various versions of 'to serve the nation, to serve humanity, to be of service to the sick'. The two girls in front of us have a hearty laugh, and we look at them not knowing why they are laughing.

'These are good stories to be read in books. Nothing like this is in reality. When you go through this grind for five and a half years, the only question on your mind would be what next? Then you have to think about admission to a postgraduate course and then how to settle and then how much you will earn. This is never ending, and it is a one way, once you are in it, you cannot turn back. It is a long process, and you will grow old getting educated. When will you get married and raise a family? You can either have a medical career or a family. We are interns and have been as foolish as you five years ago. We did not have anybody to tell us. We are telling you this out of our personal experience, if you are sensible exit. Do anything other than being a doctor, save yourself, and enjoy your life. Do you have any hobbies?'

We come up with hobbies like playing basketball, volleyball to reading and writing books to dancing and singing. 'Follow a career in one of your hobbies. You seem to be talented girls. You will not see your hobbies in this lifetime if you stay here.' Saying this, they move out as they finish eating.

It is tough to get admission in a medical college and that too in HP. We have slogged and worked hard for it, and we are right now at the top of the world since we are among the privileged few to be here. These girls are either dumb or not as smart and intelligent as us. They must have been failures in medical education and are giving free advice. *I authentically want to serve humanity, I am sure of it*, is what I am thinking. We have put our foot into the most sought after and glamorous career option in the world, and we are happy in our own ignorance of the situation we are in. We pay our respective bills and march out of the canteen, deep in thought, in different directions according to our separate destinations.

Life is like this. We meet different people in different periods of our life and then we separate and we move in different directions to meet new people and have new relationships and newer destinations. It is a continuous process. We may not meet the same people again, and sometimes we are fortunate enough to have the same people with us all the time. The more we spread love and happiness to people around us, the more fulfilled we are and the more happily we spend our lives. Thus ends my first day at HP.

We are the first ones to get admission and form the anatomy group; therefore, our roll numbers are 5, 6, 7, 8—that is Aarti, Saroj, Prachi, and me, respectively. Roll numbers 1, 2, 3, 4 is the first group consisting of Sushant, Anil, Mandar, and Deepali. We are about seventy students, and the first batch to go for dissection. We reach the dissection hall at 10.50 a.m. A strong pungent smell welcomes us, and we cover our noses and stand away from the dissection hall.

Ravi, the boy in charge of the hall, smiles on seeing our gesture. 'You will get used to this in a week's time, you will then eat your food inside,' he tells us.

We make dirty faces. Dr Jain walks in and takes us inside the hall. We go in with our noses covered with kerchiefs or dupattas. The sight inside leaves us all frail and a few fragile ones collapse. The rest of us manage to stand with support. We lean against the wall barely hearing what Dr Jain is saying. There are seven to eight embalmed dead bodies on huge tables in a large hall. Embalming is the process by which the dead bodies are preserved. The smell that we encounter is that of the embalming fluid. The dead bodies look frightening. These are unclaimed bodies or those donated by some people voluntarily.

'You will have one anatomy and one physiology lecture from 8.30 to 10.30 a.m., and you reach here after the lectures. Dissection will continue up to 1 p.m. thrice a week and then would be a tutorial with your demonstrators for an hour.'

'When do we eat?' Sushant asks the question going on in everybody's mind.

'You have entered a medical college. Eating, sleeping, and all other activities are secondary. You should be observant at all times, keen to learn, and thirsty for knowledge.' The thunderous words of Dr Jain echo in the hall.

'Lunchtime is between 2 p.m. to 3 p.m.'

The allotment of the dead bodies or cadavers, as they are called, to each group begins. We have got to dissect and study the head, face, and neck (HFN) of the body in this term. There are Aman, Nisha, Sheekha, and Arushi on our table, and they would be dissecting the lower limbs (LL). So on and so forth, there are sixteen students working on one table. We are introduced to our demonstrators. These are the people who would help us with our dissection, solve our difficulties, and conduct classes in small batches called tutorials. Everybody dissecting one part of the body on each table has one teacher or demonstrator. We are fifteen of us for HFN with Dr Jayesh Shah. We go to our table with Dr Shah, and he starts cutting the skin on the neck and gives a running commentary of what exactly he is doing. By now we have got accustomed to the smell, but we are trying to avoid looking at the sight in front of us. We keep looking at each other barring a few enthusiastic ones who are concentrating on what Dr Shah is doing, and they ask a few questions as well. Some of us do not get a clear view of what is going on since the place has become crowded. We take stools meant for sitting and stand on them. There is utter chaos all around the room when we take the first plunge into our medicine career. At around 2 p.m., we go for lunch.

The timetable shows a physiology lecture at 3 p.m. in lecture hall number two on the second floor. I am in the hall well before 3 p.m. I had previously seen classrooms which have the flooring at one level. This classroom is like a movie theatre going up the stair from the bottom upwards with rows of desks. The doors in the front open on both the sides on the second floor whereas the rear door is in the centre, opening on the third floor. We are in the first row, and our place is fixed for all lectures. There is the biochemistry lecture at 4 p.m. in the same hall.

We have physiology and biochemistry practicals alternating with the dissection in morning or the afternoon. Any given day starts at 8.30 a.m. and ends by 5.30 p.m. Life is moving at a fast pace. I come back to the hostel and study for sometime everyday. I have started liking and enjoying every bit of this life. Each day is a new day with newer challenges and with lots of innovative things to learn and experiment.

My parents speak to me on the hostel phone by placing a trunk call with the MTNL of Nashik, once in three to four days. MTNL is the telephone company of our state of Maharashtra- Maharashtra Telephone Nigam Limited. I miss them and my younger sister. At times, when I am lonely, I sit alone in the room and give vent to my tears. This is the first time I am staying away from my parents. I am getting used to the hostel food which consists of watery (dal) cooked pulses with few condiments and (sabji) vegetable with no spices and less salt. In the initial days, I would try to identify the vegetable I am eating. It turns out to be a futile exercise, and I give it up. The chapattis made of wheat or cornflour are unusually thin, small, and half-burnt or half-cooked, and the rice is never soft. Lunch at the college canteen is fun. I have different varieties of food every day. By the tenth day, I have tasted most of the items on the menu.

MBBS becomes MB. Anatomy becomes anat, physiology is shortened to physio and biochemistry to biochem. We start to get a hang of these subjects. Anat is the structural description of the body, physio is about the normal functioning mechanisms in the body, and biochem is the detailed chemical reactions happening in all the organs and systems in the human body. There are teachers who teach different systems of the body in detail. We are given notes, and we read huge books. Practical classes are real fun specially the physio practical. We are lucky being girls. The boys have to be volunteers in the practicals, at times having to strip off their shirts or fold up their trousers to demonstrate a sign or a reflex or to palpate or measure something as simple as the blood pressure. The complexities of the human body are miraculously unfolding in front of us, day by day, and week after week.

There is a notice on the board in the hostel to gather for the hostel allotment in classroom 4 at 5 p.m. the next day. I, along with the other girls from outside Mumbai, from my class, reach there on time. The room is crammed with girls wearing all types of colourful clothes with different facial features, varied statures carrying themselves in their diverse styles. The allotment of rooms begins at 4.15 p.m. when the hostel in charge, Dr Mrs Deepa, comes in. The allotment of rooms starts with the exam going final MBBS girls. They get the first preference to choose the room. The next are the second MB exam goers and then first MB exam goers. Our turn is the last. We have to choose our room-mates meanwhile.

'I am taking my best friend Poorvi as my room partner,' says Ragini.

Poonam looks at me and Simran, not knowing what to do.

'You and Simran share a room,' I say understandingly.

Just then, a tall thin girl comes near us and says expectantly, 'I am Smriti, from Jalgaon.' Her face seems familiar to me.

'I will share the room with you,' I reassure her.

Amruta is from Satara, sharing the room with Susan who hails from Ratnagiri. We meet all of them during the allotment. I am happy I have a group, and I would no longer be alone in the hostel along with the seniors. All of us are settled in our rooms within a week.

I go to Simran's room and find her reading a book. 'What are you reading?' I ask her.

'An MB.'

'I do not see you reading a medicine book.'

'Don't you know what an MB is?' she enquires.

I shrug my shoulders in the negative. She laughs aloud. Poonam enters the room and wants to know the joke. 'She does not know what an MB is.'

'It is simple. It means MBBS,' Poonam says innocently.

'Do you girls have your minds in place? I am reading a Mills and Boon novel. Have you two never heard about it?' Simran adds, looking at the perplexity on our faces. 'You have not come out of your shells, girls. You need to grow up. Well, I cannot describe the book. You better read it for yourself.' She opens a cupboard and gives us each a book with the same type of a romantic cover as the book she is reading. Thus I read the first Mills and Boon book of my life.

I have been well versed with the life at HP. Vidya, a hostel girl from my class, and I start using the fantastic library at HP. As I am about to enter the library one day, someone pulls me out.

'Hello, you do not need to study from the first term. Why don't you enjoy your life? You will anyways have to slog for the next two terms. If you do not want to enjoy, please help me complete my anat journal.' Raj is still holding my wrist while I struggle to free myself.

'Raj, my drawing is too bad. I do not even know how I would survive anat with my kind of drawing,' I tell him as a matter of fact.

'My drawing and sketching is good. I am joking. My anat journal is complete, and I have already submitted it. If you can spare some time, I will draw your sketch right now. It's one of my hobbies.'

'Raj, I have to complete my physio journal and go for the practicals in half an hour.'

'Can we do it in the evening today, Shalinii madam?'

'Raj, I am no beauty, why don't you search for a better model for your sketch?'

'You may not be beautiful, but you have sharp features and nice big eyes, that's a luxury for a painter.'

'You mean you are a painter too.'

'I am an artist, and I am passionate about getting people on paper and canvas.'

'Bye, Raj, you need to be studying.' I go and sit beside Vidya.

In the evening, I am busy reading the digestive system in the physiology book in the library, and I am astonished at the way it functions. I look up from my book to become conscious of Vidya pointing at something with her eyes. I look in the direction she is asking me to see. Raj is doing something with his head bent down. He is deeply engrossed in whatever he is doing. I smile at Vidya and get back to whatever I am reading. 'He is up to something, keeps looking in our direction every few seconds,' Vidya whispers.

'Why have you come here, to study or look at him? Why don't you concentrate on your reading?' I reprimand Vidya. After some time, I become aware of students coming inside the library, looking at us, and laughing as if seeing animals in a zoo. I feel something amiss and go out to check. I find a cartoon sketch of mine with Raj's signature at the bottom stuck on the wall outside the library door and few students surrounding it. My anger knows no bounds. Raj is nowhere in sight. A friend of his, Vishal, informs me he has gone to the hostel.

'Let's go to the boy's hostel and thrash him,' Vidya urges me.

'Forget it, Vidya. I do not want to see his face.' I cannot study later on, and I sleep without food that day.

There is this talk of the grand joons social, and there is anticipation about it in the air.

'I am not going for any social. I don't even know what it is,' I announce in the mess while eating food. Pooja is sitting nearby and overhears me. 'You have to be a part of the traditions of this college,' she proclaims. 'I would never miss such an occasion of mingling with the crowd of HP,' declares Simran.

Amruta and Susan are more than willing to go. The second-year MBBS seniors in the hostel have an emergency meeting on the fourth floor in Vidya's room as her partner is a second MBBS student. Vidya is still in the library, and Poorvi, Poonam, Smriti, and I are summoned there.

'You cannot break the rules of this hostel. We participate in every major event that happens in the non-exam-going terms, specifically the first terms of the three years. It's a matter of the prestige of this hostel. All of you have to attend the social. It is for your benefit and compulsory for all the hostelites.' I am thus being inculcated and absorbed into the HP culture.

Visits to the beauty parlours by the girls increase from one week prior to the social. There is no particular dress code, so we wear what we consider our best clothes. The venue for such events is the terrace of our college building, which has seven floors. I dress casually in a jeans and a T-shirt. Though not appropriate for the occasion, I do not want to wear anything else. Girls are in frocks and miniskirts, some wear traditional clothes. I and Vidya are standing in a corner at the party and watching the drama. The students are getting introduced to each other. Dance partners are changing every minute. There is fun and laughter all around us. We do not seem to be belonging here. All the non-exam goers are out here to welcome us. I make a quick calculation: 200 of us every year, that makes it 1,000 for five years with two exam-going batches which comes to about 600 free birds, 400 out to explore the newly joined 200 of us. We are not 600, maybe 400, which means 200 studious students studying at home, some may even be in the library. What am I doing here calculating people? An abrupt applause with some eyes darting in our direction catch my attention. As I figure out what is going on, I am encircled and escorted to the dance floor.

'Hi! What are you doing in a party? Are you a mere spectator? This party is for you. Why are you not a part of it?' I hear Raj. He is the one holding my hand. I still haven't been able to see his face owing to the crowd around us. There are too many people on the dance floor. I withdraw my hand and move out from the dance floor.

'Why are you moving away from the dance floor? I want to dance with you and be with you. I have come to see you though I have my exams. I want to introduce you to my friends. I know you would not make yourself known.'

'I do not like all this. I am at HP merely to study. My father spends a lot of money every month and takes a lot of efforts for me to be in here,' I say exasperated.

'Does that mean you do not smile? Your smile is contagious, and you seem so rigid without it. You are not even eighteen, why do you behave like a forty-year-old. You do not need to be extra mature. I was studying when Vishal came and told me how you were standing quietly at the party. I could not study, and I'm here.

'This is Shalinii, and, Shalinii, this is Ravindra Godse, our GS [general secretary of the college], and this is Vishal, my friend, and, Vishal, you know Shalinii.' He goes on talking as we meet people around. I, on my part, try to smile and say 'Hi!' to each person I meet.

I spot a person standing all alone and smoking a cigarette, away from the crowd. He seems so much like me, to me, lonely, dejected, lost. I get an impression of him as being suave and urbane. I develop an instant liking for him. He is like the guy that I have read about in the MB a few days ago. He is tall, definitely dark, and yes, handsome matches the description perfectly. It's not his looks that I adore that day, but his facial expressions; they match my inner feelings.

'Who's he, and how can he smoke here?' I ask Raj.

'Oh! He's the hottest stuff on campus, so he has to be in the hiding. Sh . . . sh . . . [Raj puts his hand on his lips gesturing me to keep quiet] Nobody is supposed to smoke here, but he is an exception. He will go to some corner and finish it in no time. You do not pay attention to him.' Saying this, Raj takes me past him.

'Would you not introduce me to him?' I ask.

'Yes, but before I do that, I need to tell you about him and do a background check about his temper today,' Raj whispers in order to prevent him from hearing us.

'Is he nasty?' I whisper back although we move out of his hearing range.

'Not really. He is known well on these grounds for his unruly manners with girls in particular.'

'Is he in your class?'

'No, he passed his first MBBS with a D in all the three subjects. He failed in pharmacology in the second year and so has an exam now.'

'What is a D?'

'Distinction.'

'A distinction in all three subjects and then failure. I don't understand. Is he sick?'

'Physically, he is healthy. Psychologically maybe. I have heard stories of a girlfriend of his who was from his class. She left him and left medicine to pursue her dream career in fashion designing. He loved her tremendously. This happened before I came to HP. I do not know more than this.'

'He should have another girlfriend.'

'Who would want to be the girlfriend of a person who hates girls?'

We are standing at the edge of the staircase, and that handsome boy crosses us and is about to go down the stairs. I nudge Raj, urging him to introduce me, by that time we are face-to-face with the man. 'This is my girlfriend, Shalinii,' Raj says to him with eagerness. He waves his hand at us in appreciation and vanishes down the stairs.

'I am not your girlfriend. How can you say this?' I express my displeasure. 'By the way, I was very angry the other day also, when you posted my cartoon on the library wall without my permission.'

'Shalinii, I like you. You think I am crazy to run behind you like this in my exam term? I liked you the day I saw you last year at the interview. You looked exceptionally innocent and out of place I could not help laughing at you. I remembered your face many times during this past one year. Secondly, he would not have even acknowledged you had I not put it that way.'

'I repeat the nth number of time—'

'That you are here to study. I know that. Okay fine, forget being my girlfriend. Can you be my friend, just friend, with no expectations and commitment?'

'That will do. It's good to have a senior as your friend to guide you in this long process of becoming a doctor.' I at last manage to smile.

'This is your unadulterated smile, and I love it. I mean pure with no added bad thoughts from your brain,' he adds, looking at the bewilderment on my face.

'I think it is time for you to go and study, and I promise I shall mingle around. Our hostel door closes sharp at 11 p.m. We have to reach before that. Good night and bye.' I see him disappear in the darkness and reach the terrace to find Susan searching for me.

'I thought we would have dinner together. Did he propose to you?' Susan asks when she sees me smiling at myself.

'Is he your boyfriend? That's what he has been bragging about in the boy's hostel. Sushant told me yesterday in the dissection hall,' adds Deepali who joins us.

The whole group bombards me with questions. 'Listen up, girls. He is not my boyfriend. He is a nice person but not my type. I like accepting challenges in life, and if I ever fall in love, it would be with somebody who really needs me in the sense nobody else can take my place there and I am indispensable. I would not actually waste myself on somebody who gets ten girlfriends like me easily.' I say all this in one deep breath and pause to breathe. Simran has come all the way from the dance floor where she has been dancing with Anil, looking at the surprised expressions on everybody's faces.

'You are crazy! Have you lost your mind? You may not meet a person like Raj ever in your life again. He is so cute, and have you seen his eyes? They are full of life. He does not even look at any other girl. You should not be breaking his heart.' It is Amruta's turn to lecture me.

'He loves you so much. I can make it out by the way he looks at you in the library. Do you know he has been coming to the library recently after you started studying there?'

'Vidya, at least I don't expect you to say this. What does he know about me? I do not know him. You and I go to the library to study, why do you have to look at him?' I try to say this as coolly as I can.

'I don't look at him. He makes it so obvious. He keeps staring at you, and I sit beside you so whenever I look up I see him.'

'Why do you have to look up while studying? I don't look up, and I don't see him,' I blast at Vidya. We are at the dining area, and we take our respective plates and start eating.

'Shalinii, do you understand? Vidya is trying to tell you that everybody else is looking at him. Simply put, he likes you, and the whole world knows about it, and he is good at his studies. Why are you against him?' Smriti's tone is persuasive.

'I know he likes me, maybe loves me. I have no such feelings for him, and I am not against him. He is a good friend, and that's it. Just because somebody very nice and good loves me, I cannot love him. I have my own priorities in life, and I am not willing to take any hasty decisions. I cannot give up my dreams for him. I am only seventeen and yet to see the world.'

'We are not asking you to give up what you want to do in life. What if he is ready to share your dreams? You are not even ready to consider and give it a thought. You should not give up easily on people. Don't cut him out of your life,' Poonam says thoughtfully.

It is five minutes to eleven; we have finished our dinner, and we run to our abode in silence and enter the gate to find the watchman with the lock in his hands approaching the main door.

'Thanks, girls, you care for me, and it indeed means a lot. I did not know before coming here that I would have a wonderful family so soon. I did not plan to have friends till this day. I do not need anyone and could live on my own is what I always thought.' I hug Poonam, Simran, Smriti, Amruta, Ragini, Poorvi, Vidya, and Susan and with moist eyes bid each of them good night before we go to our respective rooms. It is the beginning of a bond developing which would last forever.

We always exist in a society, a group, a family. Put a man in a big villa with all the luxuries, food, wealth, books, music, but no other human being. His happiness would be short–lived, and he would long for company, for friendship, for love. We cannot exist alone. Loneliness is the biggest reason for depression in humans in the whole world. If we keep aside our egos, our conversations about other people, and accept any other person as our own self, we would have peace and harmony in our lives. The problem is we do not accept and are not fine with the way we ourselves are. We are our own biggest critics. Criticism is good at times for our progress. It becomes a hindrance to our evolution when we overdo it. A person who is not at peace with one's own self cannot be at peace with anybody and anything. Internal harmony brings external tranquillity. Equilibrium within is stability outside. We are at the centre of the ripple that emanates from us, surrounds us and extends far and wide. What to transmit through the ripple is a matter of our choice.

CHAPTER SIX

There is a blood donation camp at HP. There are students volunteering to donate blood and collect blood from donors. I am in the queue for donating blood.

The guy I had been introduced to, by Raj on the staircase, on the day of the social was helping in the blood collection process. He spots me and says, 'Haven't you joined the college recently? You are not even eighteen, plus you stay in the hostel and eat non-nutritious food. You cannot donate blood. Your weight is 44 kilograms, the minimum weight required for a person to give 350 millilitres of blood is 45 kilograms. You are not fit to donate blood. Leave immediately.' He sounds very rude to me.

'But my haemoglobin is above 11, and I am told that is the only criteria for donating blood. I want to donate blood,' I insist.

'Vishal, can you go and call Raj? She would not listen to us,' he calls aloud while opening a blood bag for a donor's blood collection.

I am furious by then, and I yell, 'What has Raj got to do with me donating blood? It is none of his business.'

'Raj is your boyfriend and a friend of mine. If you have any problem, I am answerable to him. The truth is you are not eligible for blood donation, and I am calling the person whom I think you will listen to.'

'Raj is not my boyfriend, and if I have made up my mind to donate blood, I will donate it, you or Raj cannot stop me from doing that. Raj told you I am his girlfriend since he believed you would not recognize me if he does not formally present me to you as that.'

'I know Raj from the day he joined this college. He stays next to my room in the boys' hostel. He is not the one who would be interested in flirting with girls. Unless you are someone special for him, he would not even talk to you. You should consider yourself lucky for having him as a part of your life. The problem with you girls is that you woo a guy and then do not want to commit or go in for a long-term relationship. You remember your parents and uncles and aunts and the society and what not later on.' He speaks with bitterness and coldness in his tone.

'I am here to donate blood and not talk to you about Raj and me. Can we discuss this some other time?' The assertiveness in my voice makes him give up, and he pushes me onto a bed and before I know what he is up to, I feel a sharp pain in my left arm as the needle pierces my skin and blood begins to flow out. I then become numb to any sensation and close my eyes. I get a nauseated feel and I abruptly open my eyes. He is busy working but does not miss the startled look on my face. He walks towards me instantly and looks enquiringly. I keep staring back at him.

'Do you have some problem? Are you fine? Do you want me to remove this needle? Does it hurt too much?' There is genuine concern in his tone, and I am speechless looking at the kind and tender expression on his face. I do not deem him to be the same person who was yelling at me moments ago. I feel some heavenly connection with this man standing in front of me. In reply to all his questions, I answer back by smiling sweetly. I lay back on the bed silently thereafter giving him an impression that all is well. He moves away from me and continues with whatever task he is doing prior to my interference. We are both aware of the watchful eyes we have on each other. We meet some people and develop an instant liking for them. Why? I cannot answer this question. I am at a loss to understand the familiarity that I feel for this stranger. I wonder why I like him. My blood collection is about to get over. He measures my blood pressure before removing the needle. I wince with the pain and sigh. He pats me caringly on my shoulder and holds my hand to help me sit up. I do not feel like letting go of his hand. He finally withdraws it and gets biscuits and coffee for me. Biscuits and coffee are essentially served by the ward boys. I thank him and am about to leave the blood bank when I hear him say, 'You are indeed a brave girl. You stay here all alone and still you dare to do such a noble service. Take care.' There is too much of softness hidden under the tough exterior.

My first term is over. I do not know how the time passed away. We have the Diwali vacation, and I go to Nashik with five heavy bags full of books. Our first term exam starts after the vacations. We from the hostel explore many of the markets in Mumbai to take gifts for our families at home. I travel alone for the first time in my life with luggage which is beyond me to carry. The train and bus reservations are full. The happiness of going home makes me overcome all impediments.

I am in Nashik, and I enjoy the vacation. I meet old friends and relatives. 'You have lost weight,' my mother comments as soon as she sees me.

'You were not there to cook for me,' I say and hug her. Both of us cry. I rest, eat, and study if time permits. I remember and talk to my parents about the girls in the hostel, keeping in mind not to comment anything about the boys. I visit the holy places and temples in Nashik and go for picnics to nearby places with my friends.

My father comes to leave me to Mumbai as my vacation ends. We return to the hostel, each of us two kilograms heavier than what we had been before going home. We have viva, practical exams, and theory exams starting in two days. Each of us is trying to judge whether the others have studied or not. We have lunch, with food packed by our moms, sitting in one of the rooms together on the first day. We talk about our holidays and a chance discussion makes us aware that all of us are sailing in the same boat—None of us have focused on our studies.

Whenever we are guilty of not having done enough or of not being up to the mark, we regret, feel bad. We blame ourselves for not giving our best. The moment we make out that we are not the only ones with the default mode of functioning, that we have company, our agony becomes less severe. This is the herd mentality we are born with. We repent at our shortcomings in life but feel good when somebody else is bad or worse than us. We give too much importance to ourselves and do not like anybody doing better than us. Many things are done by us to show people around what we are capable of. We like to look down on others. Our actions are given by what people relate to us as or what we want them to relate to us as. We are not free beings. God has given us brains to think about the good and bad in general about our race, the human race. We use our brains more often to find new ways of pushing others down and rising high up, high up on the ladder of success. Can all of us rise up the ladder of the so-called success together? For us to rise up, we need not push somebody down. It is easy to do that. We need to shift the focus from ourselves to things and people around us. As we strive for others, we are shifting to an entirely new level of growth, satisfaction, and happiness. When we struggle for others, it is not our struggle, and we perform better as the end result no longer matters to us. Similarly if the end result anyways does not matter to us, we become better performers in our life too.

We go searching for some senior to explain us the pattern of the exams. We find Tanvi studying in her room. 'What does a viva mean and how is it conducted?' I ask her.

'Viva is an oral exam. The examiner asks you questions on a topic and then you should be able to lead the examiner,' Tanvi informs us.

'What is leading the examiner?' This is Amruta's query, and all of us want to know it, so we bob our heads in agreement with her.

'The examiner asks you a question, you answer it in such a way that he goes on to a topic you know well. Instruments and specimens are also kept there for you to speak and elaborate on. They might give you an instrument or you could get a choice to pick up a specimen to discuss, and you can tactfully and skillfully manoeuvre your talk onto a topic you have studied well. You therefore have to prepare accordingly.'

'This seems impossible. How can you guide the examiner?' Smriti asks astonished.

'It is a matter of time, I mean with experience you will learn to direct your talk to the subject of your liking. One more thing is very important in vivas. If you do not know the answer to some question, say I do not know. Do not waste your time. You can move on to the other topics and score well,' Tanvi informs us.

We go to our respective rooms and try to study with the new guidelines of studying we have received. The pressure of the exams is mounting with the passing time. We cannot concentrate, and we go to each other's rooms for support. After dinner, Poorvi, Poonam, Smriti, and Amruta sit together in our room to study. I am an early riser and cannot study at night. I go to sleep at 10 p.m. I wake up at 5 a.m. to find the four of them asleep in different positions on the chairs and the table. I wake them up and ask them to sleep properly at least for some time in their respective beds.

The exams are a taste of what medical education is, for us. The results are not declared; however, most of us are aware where we stand. We, the toppers of the best junior colleges of the state of Maharashtra, fumble, jumble, muddle, clutter, and invent confusion. We feign ignorance when we know in our hearts that we have been in the euphoria and overconfidence of having got admission into HP. Our seniors tell us that this is also a part of HP's legend. The exams make an important change in our attitude towards looking at it. The casualness of the first term vanishes, and we are no more grand joons. We belong here, and we have a responsibility—responsibility towards ourselves, our families, our college, our teachers, and the nation at large.

Responsibility is a relative term. Its meaning varies from person to person. For some people, it means blame or liability; others would attribute it to accountability or a job or a task. It could be dependability for some and conscientiousness for a few. When we use responsibility in the above contexts, it is a big burden, a heavy weight we have to carry on our shoulders, and we tend to shun away from it, evade it. It gives us a bad feeling, and we are addicted to the feel-good factor. Responsibility can be to know for ourselves who we are and what we are up to in our lives. A cinema has characters whose roles in it are predefined and predetermined. By being responsible, we simply write our role in this big live cinema called life. In short, we write our own destiny, our own fate, by being responsible.

While coming back to our residence on the last day of our exams, Ragini is on the top of the world. 'It's over at last. I have slept for just four hours each day. I shall go to sleep. Don't wake me for dinner.' Poorvi agrees to her plan of action instantly.

'You are like twin sisters. One is at all times with the other. How do you manage to live in such perfect synchrony with each other?' I say amazed by the communion they share.

'It's easy, Shalinii. I do what Ragini wants to do, and she respects my wishes. We think about the other before ourselves.'

'I am tired, not sleepy at all. Even if I try to sleep, I will not be able to. I would read a book, and Simran will definitely read an MB.' Poonam who's a book worm, says this.

'I want to go have a nice bath. I skipped it today morning. A nice hot shower will help me rejuvenate and get me out of the stress and strain of the exams.' Smriti pitches in.

'I have a headache, girls, and I am hungry too. I have been fasting each day since our exams. I have had meals once a day all along these days,' says Amruta.

'Come on, friends, it's just a small college exam, and you are worked up because of it. Let's enjoy today before we seriously start studying tomorrow onwards. Let's go to Marine Lines, take the pleasure of watching the sea and have dinner at a fancy restaurant.' I say excitedly.

'Give us half an hour to complete the tasks we listed and we will move out of the hostel.' Amruta represents the group.

We are at the station in an hour. Girls always take time to get ready and especially when going out. While routinely going to the college every morning in a haste, we do not bother to dress up formally or put some make-up on. It's not the same when we are moving out of the campus. We have an excellent time at the seashore. The cool breeze helps calm our nerves. We marvel at the setting sun, after many days. We converse with each other and the sea. The weariness and exhaustion of the exams disappear, and we are fresh as if at the beginning of life. We pledge to ourselves that this would indeed be the actual beginning of our medical career.

We are naive and new to the city of Mumbai. While returning back to our hostel, we take eight tickets of the local train. We decide to have food at Swad Hotel near our college. On the platform, when the train approaches, five of us manage to get in, and we are pulling at two others when the train starts. Amruta is still on the platform. We let go of Ragini and Smriti as well.

'Should we get off at the coming station and travel together in the next train?' I ask the others.

'No, it will not be easy searching for their compartment. We better go ahead and wait for them at the station after we reach our destination,' says Simran.

'The tickets are with Amruta,' I comment. Simran immediately puts a hand on her mouth asking me to shut up.

'Oh! What if the ticket checker asks us for tickets? We will be caught and punished for travelling without tickets,' whispers an aggrieved Poonam.

'Nobody will know that we do not have our tickets with us, we will not exit the station,' Simran tries to pacify us.

We get down at our destination. There is no ticket checker in site, and Simran guides us out of the station and says, 'It is better to stand outside rather than inside.' We wait for the remaining three of us for half an hour which extends to an hour of waiting. There is no sign of them. We are at a loss as to the whereabouts of our friends.

'Let's go check if they have gone to Swad directly. They might have come by a fast train and gone ahead of us,' I say.

'Two of you go to Swad, and the rest of us will wait here. If they have reached there, come back to inform us and if they come here, we will bring them there.' The final word is Simran's.

I and Poonam go to Swad. We search the whole place. The people seated in the hotel keep looking at us. They must be wondering what we are up to. 'They are not here,' I declare after a thorough search.

'Could they be at the hostel?' Poonam questions.

'Let's go and check there,' I speak my mind.

We reach the hostel to find none of them there. We go back to the hotel once again to see if all of them have arrived. They are not at the hotel. We reach the station to find our friends standing right at the entrance. They are without the three girls. 'What took you so long?' Simran is visibly angry.

'We even checked at the hostel. They are not to be found,' I tell everyone.

'Could they have gone to some other place?'

'They would not. They know we would be looking for them.'

'It's been almost three hours since the time we are awaiting their return. Let's go to the hostel. There is no point in standing here.'

We go and sit in the TV room. None of us is watching the television though. It is 10.30 p.m., and we start to panic. Our gate will close in half an hour, and there is no sign of our missing friends. I go to Pooja's room for advice. She has a night emergency and is in the hospital. Next I go to Tanvi for help.

'Should we lodge a missing persons complaint with the police?' I ask her.

'No, you will first have to inform the hostel warden. You cannot directly go to the police. It has to be through proper channels. The dean needs to be informed next. I will come with you to the warden's room. Don't worry, they would be safe, must have gone shopping someplace.'

As we are coming down the stairs, our missing friends enter the hostel gate at five minutes to eleven. All of us surround them and are worried, looking at their worn-out faces.

'We got into the first-class compartment by mistake and were caught by the ticket checker (TC) while getting down. He took us to the station master's office. When we told them that it was a mistake and we were new to Mumbai, they would not listen. They thought we regularly travelled by first class on a second-class ticket. We even showed them the eight tickets and explained how we were left behind. They did not budge and asked us to pay the first-class fare. We did not have that much money. We showed them our identity cards. We also asked them to let one of us go to fetch money. They did not allow that too. We reasoned with them and requested them to give us some concession. According to them, we should have got down and changed the compartment at the next station. We never realized we were in the wrong compartment. They agreed at last but took it in writing from us that henceforth we will not repeat this mistake. They charged us for three tickets and only for the next three stations instead of five, and we are here.' Smriti narrated their woe tale.

'You should have called up at the hostel,' Tanvi says.

'They would not let us call up from their phone.' Mobile phones did not exist in India then.

We learn a lesson that day. We decide not to venture out of the campus too often and to stick to each other under any circumstances. Local trains can turn out to be unsafe, more so during rush hours. We should carry enough money if we have to go anyplace out of the campus. Good times can turn into bad at any moment. This is the city of Mumbai, and anything can crop up here at anytime.

The library opens sharp at eight in the morning. Vidya and I reach there at that time and keep our bags to reserve our seats before going for our first lecture. We have no practical that day and come back to our seats in the afternoon. We find Raj sleeping on the chair with his head resting on the table across my chair. 'He recognizes your bag,' whispers Vidya.

'It's just a coincidence,' I whisper back. I issue a book from the librarian and start reading it. I cannot concentrate on reading. Raj is snoring at our table. I put my head up and spot the blood donation fellow sitting behind Raj facing us. My eyes meet his, and we smile. This gets repeated three times. I am tempted by some unknown force to look at him and find him looking at me. It becomes hard for me to concentrate further. Every few minutes, we look at one another. I at last drag Vidya out of the library. 'I cannot study here. Let's go and study in the hostel.'

Vidya is reluctant; she says, 'The moment I go to my room and see the bed, I feel like going off to sleep.'

'We will read in the reading room of the hostel,' I tell her.

'It was you who insisted on studying in the library this morning, why do you have a problem now?'

'There is no problem. I am sleepy,' I lie to her, and we go to the hostel.

I decide against going to the library at all. I find a lady staying nearby to give me home-cooked packed lunch in the hostel. This is to prevent myself from going to the canteen. I come to the hostel for lunch and go back for my classes. I do not know what and whom I am avoiding. I become a recluse though.

There have been times when I have been homesick, and I miss my parents, sister, neighbours, and friends. I would cry in the lectures. We have a professor in the Department of Anatomy who believes in non-formal education. We would have singing and joke sessions during his lectures. He would disburden us off our studies and worries. His way of teaching us is unique. Nobody would forget the basic anatomy he taught us for a long time to come. He is a fine orator and speaker. He has knowledge about a lot of subjects, and he is well read. He would teach us by giving literary examples, a rare combination of arts with science. We would look forward to the lectures of Dr Kothari. I personally would unleash and give vent to all my pent up negative emotions during his lectures, which would liberate me, enthuse me and charge me up to deal with all my problems effectively.

The rose day is announced in the college and all the students are thrilled. 'What is a rose day?' I ask Poonam.

'It is an expression of love and friendship through roses. There are different colours of roses for different purposes like a red rose for love and a yellow one for friendship.'

'Why are roses required to express love and friendship, and why a particular day?' is my query.

'You see, people do not have a lot of time in a city like Mumbai. Sometimes they are shy and cannot express themselves,' she explains.

'I find it ridiculous. We do not have time for basic things like love and friendship. I think they are feelings to be felt day in and day out. Is it that people in Mumbai store their feelings and then vomit them out on this day? It seems artificial, unnatural. When you talk about shyness and timidity, I think our generation is quite bold, plus what is the foundation of a relationship which has its beginning with these?' I am displeased.

'You have to experience it to understand what it is. You will see so many couples being formed and broken from this day onwards. A girl with the maximum number of roses becomes the rose queen' is her reply to my immaturity.

The rose day arrives, and I find all the girls in their best attire and make-up. After all the lectures are over, the announcement of the roses begins in our classroom. Ragini receives the maximum number of roses and is the rose queen. She is very sweet and beautiful. The next is Poonam who is very popular in the class. She is indeed chivalrous, loving and caring. The rest of us get two to three roses each. I receive a yellow rose from Raj. Two more yellow roses from Mandar and Aarti and an unknown red rose. This is the only rose in the whole class which has no sender's name. There are lots of speculations. Most of my friends feel it is Raj who sent it to me and did not reveal his name as he would not want to rub me the wrong way so that I do not put him in my bad books. Their doubts disappear when Anil, who is the class representative and in charge of the rose day, tells me that it came from a senior, but it is not Raj.

CHAPTER SEVEN

The college festival is round the corner. We are all studying seriously, and we have exams every now and then. I find this festival a distraction. I decide to have a taste of it at least once. Preparations begin well in advance. We are given the task of getting sponsorships for the three-day program. We go in groups of four to bring in sponsors. Students who know industrialists and celebrities bring in big money easily. The rest of us have to struggle to get smaller amounts of money. I learn about the money psychosis that people have during this time.

At the places that we visit, we are called in immediately after we send in our identity cards. When we ask them for money and their advertisement, people are hesitant. If we are out to do some charitable work and they get an income tax benefit, they do not mind helping us. They are willing to invest for a noble cause. Sponsorship of a college function seems beyond their imagination. After experiencing reluctance on their part, we stop sending in our identity cards. We are not entertained at all thereafter.

'Let's modify our talk. We just tell them that we have our college magazine, and we would advertise their product in it plus an additional benefit of making their product known during our college function, I suggest.'

'Will that really help?' Mandar, who is a member of my team, says.

'Why not give it a try. I do not know how these marketing guys sell their products. They convince their customers very well. I am at a loss of how to convince people about what we are doing.' This is Vidya's comment.

'I have heard from a distant uncle of mine that medical practice is arts, commerce plus science. Once we finish our MBBS course, we have to manage all the three. We are taught only science in the college and through our books. Rest of the two skills we have to develop on our own. The success of a medical practitioner depends not on the science as we all learn the same things here. It depends on the other two branches. It is how well we manage to sell ourselves, that is how well we can convince people how good we are. We may be very good at our diagnosis and our knowledge about the subject, but if the patient does not understand or agree to what you are saying, you are a bad doctor. You should be able to put through your knowledge across to the patient at the level of their understanding, along with the preconceived notions they have about their illness.'

I am zapped by these comments by Anil, my fourth colleague. 'How do you know so much? You are saying that we do our MBBS in these five and a half years, then a postgraduate course of three to six years depending on specialty or super specialty and face criticism for no fault of ours. People will judge our talking skills.'

'My uncle is an orthopaedic surgeon. He tells me all these things. You slog to learn and gather knowledge, and there would be somebody with no degree or proper education practicing next to you and at times telling patients what you are prescribing is wrong.'

'How can that be possible? People do understand the qualifications,' I counter.

'People take their health for granted and the cheapest thing is human life in India. Money tops the list of priority and the next is food, clothing, own vehicle, house or land, flamboyant lifestyle. They rush to the hospital at the eleventh hour and would look at you as if you gave them the illness. If there is a complication because of their coming late to you or as a result of the disease per se, it is your inefficiency,' Anil says.

'Yes, I comprehend there are many shortcuts to being a medical practitioner and everybody's conscience is not as clear as you and me.'

'I am not going to stay in this country. I am going to go to the US as soon as I finish my MBBS.'

'Anil, what is the point in running away like this?' I question him.

'You have no experience about the life of doctors there. In the US, doctors are treated with respect and dignity. They not only earn well but have a very good lifestyle with fixed working hours. I am not wasting myself where I have no recognition for my work.'

Money is the ultimate goal of all *Homo sapiens*. It is true; money can buy everything. I am yet to determine whether money can give me peace of mind, satisfaction, and happiness. These are states of the mind. A person may live in a palace and not be happy, and a person living in a hut could be a master of his life. Money should be gotten but by fair means, not at the expense of some other person. When a man is clear-hearted and can go to sleep without the worries of tomorrow or the worries of his own wrong doings, he is peaceful. If a wealthy man can be himself without all his wealth and a poor man can be himself even if he acquires all the wealth in the world, money automatically becomes powerless and man ultimately becomes powerful. A man who has nothing but a strong vision can go miles ahead of the rest.

Two days prior to the festival, we are in the dissection hall dissecting the path of the ulnar nerve of the hand. Prachi asks me, 'Shalinii, do you have a senior as your room-mate, and how many of you stay in one room?'

'We are just two of us in one room, Smriti and me,' I answer.

'What time do you two sleep? How big is your room?' This question is asked by Aarti.

It is Saroj's turn to ask before I answer Aarti, 'Do you have extra beds in your rooms?'

'Why are you three asking me these questions all of a sudden?' I counter-question them instead of giving a straight answer.

'Actually we are thinking . . .' Saroj glances at the other two.

I have no idea of what they want, and I get irritated. 'Tell me what is wrong. Are you up to a prank? Why are you hesitating? If you need some help, you do not even have to ask. I am there for you.'

'We want to stay in the hostel during the college festival so that we can enjoy it till late in the night.'

'Oh! You are most welcome. We are buddies, and naturally, I can share my room with you all.'

The festival is grand. It is like a Bollywood majestic event. A red carpet is placed all over the place. CCTV cameras are installed to monitor the whole college premises. A huge rangoli with varied colours adorns the entrance each day. Flowers and garlands are seen everywhere. It is like HP has become a bride for three days. The event is inaugurated by film stars, and there are celebrities from every walk of life to boost the celebrations. Students belonging to two hundred different colleges from all over the city attend the festival. It is a magnificent success, and it leaves an everlasting impression on our minds.

We have all the lectures scheduled on time except during the college festival. In anatomy, we have only the lower limbs remaining to be studied. We are done with the rest of the body. The most complicated structures to study are, like we all know, the heart and the brain. A newer introduction in this term is histology, which is the study of the detailed tissue structure at the cellular level. There are a lot of diagrams in this, and we would go to the library each day to complete them. All of us reach the library at the same time and make a lot of noise. As there are many dots in the diagrams, we all make a *tuck tuck tuck* sound with the pencil while putting the dots, and we are driven out of the library one day. Histology also means being under the microscope during each lecture. It would give me headache at times.

In physiology, we have finished most of the systems except the reproductive and the nervous systems. Here also the heart and the brain rule. Mrs Dahale starts teaching us the reproductive system in detail. We come to the sex act one day. Mrs Dahale in her loud voice is teaching us the sex act and we, 200 of us, adult students do not dare to put our heads up. We are embarrassed when she is very boldly telling us the intricacies of the sexual act. There is pin-drop silence in the class. We have never before been introduced to this in our life. There is no medium for us to have this knowledge. We feel as if it would be better if the earth opens up and swallows us. It is here that we learn how we have been born. Even after the lecture is over, we cannot have an eye-to-eye contact with most of our classmates. All of us just disappear to have food.

Biochemistry has a number of complicated chemical reactions that we have to remember. The reactions are again at the cellular level, and it is a wonder how so many things can happen at that stage. There is coordination in the three subjects, and we get a complete big picture of our marvellous body. It is a design the best of engineers would not have been able to design. Forget the design; replication is also not possible for man. Many people are not proud to have a human body. We are the most complicated and exclusive thing the earth has. Is that not enough for us to rejoice and celebrate each day of our existence on this planet?

We have exams, exams, and exams now and then. Time flies off fast, and our second term comes to an end. We have a one-month summer vacation in the college before the exams, and we go home. Before long the second-term exams are also over. We long for the clinical terms which start from the second year. Prior to going to the second year of MBBS, we have to cross the hurdle of the first MBBS final exams. We are in the third semester of the first year of MBBS the exam term.

There is this exam fever in the air. Most of us study in the library. Vidya sits in the library from 8 a.m. when it opens to 10 p.m., the time of its closure. We talk studies, we eat studies, and we sleep studies. We do not become conscious of the fact that the grand joons have joined. We have no time to know whether the sun is rising in the east or the west; is it a sunny or a rainy day? Sometimes we are not aware of whether it is day or night. Each of us has a unique style of studying.

'I like to read as many books as possible on a particular topic, like reading a storybook or novel, to gather knowledge,' I say while having lunch one day. We are now on a study leave of absence from the college. All of us take food from my dabba lady staying near our hostel who would supply us fresh, hot, home-cooked food. We would gather in one room and have lunch together. It would be a nice break, and we would gossip and be rejuvenated to study in the next session.

'I prepare proper point-wise notes to make reading at the last moment easier,' says Simran.

'I sit with the past question papers and prepare answers accordingly. Anyways the questions get repeated, so I know how to write the exact answer and score more.' This is Amruta who likes shortcuts in life.

'I am in love, friends,' announces Vidya.

'What are you talking about? Who has taken advantage of the fact that I am not coming to the library with you? This is no time for love. You should be studying now. I am sure you met him in the library,' I say.

'You are right. We would study in the library, he and me, and we would go to the canteen together for breakfast, lunch, and dinner since the past few days. I had no one to have food with,' Vidya answers.

'I was telling Shalinii the other day that something is amiss with you. I have seen you on the phone every now and then. Shalinii would not believe me. She was sure she would have known.' This is Smriti who had discussed this with me in the room two days ago.

'I am sorry, Shalinii, but I was myself not sure of anything. He proposed me yesterday, and I have not yet answered him. I want your opinion.'

'First let us know who it is. Is the person worth your affection? We will then decide about the proposal. How could you fall in love? I do not think I shall ever fall in love. I do not even want to get married.'

'Shalinii, you have the right to know who it is. First tell me, why do you not want to get married?'

'We do not have time for it right now. You tell us the name of the person.'

Smriti puts in, 'Can I guess? Is it Mandar?'

'Yes, it is. How do you know?'

'I overheard you taking his name while speaking to him on the phone a few days ago. I received his phone, when he had called you up on the landline phone of the hostel yesterday and recognized his voice.'

I am in for a real surprise. 'You mean Mandar from our class? He is a very decent and sober guy. I think you should accept his proposal. Have the two of you gone mad? We have our exams approaching in another fortnight, and you are singing love songs. The next time he calls you, ask him not to call you again or inform him that you would decide after the exams, or better still hand over the phone to me when he calls up and I shall do the talking.' I go into an elder sister mode.

'Shalinii, he said if I say yes, he would be able to concentrate on his studies better. He expects me to answer him as early as possible.'

'What is the problem then? You can commit to him for a lifetime relationship, maybe marriage.

'I need to think a bit, ask my parents, how can I suddenly rush into a relationship? I have known him only recently.'

'Tell him you accept his proposal for now, don't talk to him until after the exams, and then decide.'

'That is indeed a good idea.' Everyone agrees to my suggestion.

Our lunch is over. Vidya, Smriti, and I go down to the study room. We are bored of looking at the same walls, doors, windows, tables and chairs in our respective rooms. We study in the hostel study room all afternoon, eat snacks, drink tea in the mess, in the evening and then go to our rooms. Our favourite pastime these days is to eat whenever we are tired of studying. I have never known I can be so hungry, and I have such a good appetite. Each of us is gaining weight day by day.

The big exam fuss is over. We are like free birds. It is the last vacation we would get to go home. We will have to await our results and begin the second year. Next we would have clinical terms, so there would be no vacation. We would have to attend the wards. All of us are fed up of just reading books. We want to examine actual patients.

We have become a family, the nine of us, specifically Vidya, Smriti, Amruta, and I are inseparable. We visit the Titwala Ganesha temple before going home. We go on a shopping spree to make purchases for everyone at home. On the last day of our stay in Mumbai, we go to the college canteen for lunch. The moment we sit, Mandar comes and joins us. Vidya is a bit uncomfortable.

'Welcome, Mandar. How are you? Have you come to meet Vidya? We have been busy with our shopping for the past few days.' I break the ice. Vidya has not communicated with him since our exams got over.

'I came to your hostel a couple of times, but you all were not there. I was not sure whether you have left Mumbai or not.'

'We are leaving tonight,' Vidya blurts out all of a sudden.

'Oh! Can you give me your residence phone number, Vidya? I can talk to you sometimes,' he says sadly.

'Vidya, since we have not ordered our food yet, can we shift to another table?' Smriti is at a loss as the conversation becomes Vidya oriented. She feels they should be able to talk privately. Mandar agrees to it, but Vidya pulls at my dress from below the level of the table so that Mandar cannot see what she is doing. I look up; I see Vidya requesting us to stay back with her eyes. So I sit down. Smriti and Amruta are unaware of this, and they go and sit on the next table. Before I could say a word to them, we have one more visitor on our table. Raj comes and sits on the chair just vacated by Smriti.

'Is something serious going on here, or have I come at the wrong time?' he asks me.

'Mandar, Vidya likes you as a person, she loves you too. She is but not ready for a commitment at present. Whatever she said to you before was to not disturb you during the exams. What she requires is just some time. She also wants the approval of her parents before taking any final decision,' I say, ignoring Raj and his question as if he does not exist.

'You girls have a problem, man. What have your parents got to do with your relationships?' Raj speaks before Mandar could react.

'Raj, we do not want your expert comments. It is between the two of them. Let them decide the future course of their friendship.' I have done my job having said this. I hold Raj by his arm and pull him on to his legs, taking him to join Amruta and Smriti on their table. My grip is tight, and it is tough for Raj to resist.

'You are very strong. You actually lifted me and brought me here. What do you eat?' Raj is completely shaken. Amruta and Smriti, who have been watching us, have a nice laugh at Raj's expense.

'I think we need to shift table again,' says Amruta to Smriti, eyeing Raj.

'Oh! No! I saw you all and came to say hi and bye. Wouldn't you be leaving for your vacation soon? How have your exams been? It is a silly question to ask, isn't it?' Raj answers his own question.

'How are your clinical terms going on? You would be exam-going next term. How are the subjects of the second year?' Smriti asks Raj.

'In the second year, we have microbiology, pharmacology, pathology, and forensic medicine. These are the basis on which the clinical subjects stand. Microbiology is the detailed study of the various microorganisms. Pharmacology, as the name suggests, is everything regarding all the drugs available under the sky. Pathology is the opposite of physiology—that is, you learn the normal processes of the body in physiology. What happens in a diseased state is what you learn in pathology. Forensic is the medico-legal aspect of medicine. The subjects are interesting, and you can study for your third year alongside while doing the clinical terms.'

'Thanks for the information, Raj,' Smriti says.

'I have to attend my pharmac practical. I need to move. But before I go, Shalinii, do you mind giving me your phone number?'

'You will have to place a trunk call. I am not sure STD facilities have reached there or not.'

'STD just started two days ago in your city, and the code for your place is 0253.'

'Thanks for the information. The phone number at my house is 23533.'

'Will your parents mind if I call you up?'

'That will depend on how frequently you call. If you call once in a while, they will not mind.'

Raj is lost in his thoughts for a minute or two. He quickly regains himself and says, 'Bye, girls, see you after you come back. Enjoy your last vacation.' He gets up and runs for the stairs of the canteen since he is late.

'Bye, Raj,' all of us say at the same time.

Amruta keeps looking over her back until he disappears. 'I somehow like this boy. He is always thorough with his knowledge. I have seen him explaining topics to others and solving their difficulties. He is known as the Good Samaritan of his class. Girls go to him with problems just to be with him.'

'Yes, he is a gem of a person and a gentleman. He is always smiling. I am yet to see him in a bad temper,' is Smriti's input.

'Whom are you talking about? Is it Raj?' This is a question by Vidya who joins us. 'I do not understand why you have a dilemma, Shalinii? You have to share your secret of not getting married, with us today. Do you remember your promise before the exams?' she further adds.

'There is nothing undisclosed. What do you expect to hear, that I have some covert affair with a mysterious person? Yes, I do have an affair, but it is with my principles in life. I am a socialite. I want to be a people's person. You know how men are possessive about their girlfriends and wives. Who would tolerate this? Secondly, I do not want children of my own. When there are so many lives struggling to live on this earth, why should I give birth to a baby? It is better to give a new life to somebody who is already born, already existing. The world anyways is not such a good place to live in. I do not want to get my children into this bad world.'

We hear somebody clapping hands and the words 'Very original and innovative thoughts you have. Superb, I am yet to meet a person like you. You think yourself to be some saint or Mahatma? It's a privilege to know you. Wow! My day has been done'. There is a feeling of mockery in those words, and a loud laughter fills the air around us. I am taken aback for a moment. Slowly I turn my back to see who has overheard our conversation as the voice comes from behind me. The voice seems known, but the frowns on the faces of Amruta and Vidya, sitting across me who could see the person concerned, convey otherwise.

It is the Blood Bank guy. I had guessed so, though I was not so sure. I remember Raj's words and I smile. I say, 'Hello! How are you?'

My friends are in a state of total confusion and shock. They do not know this person, and they think I am at my wits' end to be smiling and enquiring politely of a person who has made me and my thoughts look foolish.

'I never imagined you to be so dumb, Shalinii. I respect you as somebody courageous, but you seem to be paranormal, no wonder you do not want to be with a normal person like Raj.' He continues doing what he is so well known for, ridiculing and teasing women. 'By the way, why did you stop studying in the library? I have been missing you a lot.'

My friends are astonished, and they look at me with questioning eyes. Before I have a chance to say something to them, he continues his mischievous trend, 'She has not spoken to you all her dear, dear friends, about me. We have crossed lines a number of times, she and I, to be separated again by time. Beware of this minuscule being and her petite brain with big thoughts. She recently demonstrated her strength when Raj was with you all.' He has been eavesdropping on us since Raj was with us.

It is my turn to be discomfited, and I am bitter and angry at this humiliation. I shout at the top of my voice, 'What do you think of yourself? Are you some Hollywood superstar? I do not even know your name. Yes, I have known you since Raj introduced you as his friend, and yes, unfortunately we have met each other a few times which does not mean I have anything to do with you.'

'*Shh shh*. Why are you making a scene here? I am just trying to be friendly and getting acquainted with your friends. I have unnecessarily felt at fault as I wondered whether you stopped coming to the library because of me. I have been searching for you to say sorry, but I could not find you all these days. When I once asked Raj, he said you were busy studying at the hostel. I really am sorry if I may have hurt you now or previously. Bye.' He vanishes from the canteen instantly.

'I do not know him. Like he said, I have met him twice or thrice,' I say avoiding the treacherous glances on my friends' faces.

'I comprehend why you stopped coming to the library, all of a sudden. Is he not the same guy who would sit on the table right across ours? I recollect he would keep looking at you occasionally.' The first to remark is Vidya.

'I did not stop studying in the library because of some person. I like to lie down on my bed and study. I was also fed up of the canteen food.'

'He indeed is nothing short of a Hollywood hero. How did we not notice him before, Smriti?' Amruta asks Smriti, who has got into Amruta's habit of being fascinated by good-looking men.

'You are undeniably one lucky girl. Two of the best guys on campus have their eyes on you, and you are unperturbed by their attention.'

'Nobody is paying me any extra attention, and my goals in life are very diverse. As I was saying formerly, I am not the one who would get tied to a man and give up my identity and individuality for a family. I am not made out to listen to and follow any person. I love my freedom and independence.'

'What if you find that somebody, who would not compromise your liberty and free will?' Smriti who has been a silent spectator adds her views.

'No man can tolerate a female's autonomy and sovereignty. Even if any such man does exist, he would be bound by his family of mother, father, siblings, the society, our culture. How long would he be able to walk by my side is a question which we better not answer. I guess we are late, we have to pack our bags too, let's get moving.' I toddle off, and the rest of them follow, each disconnected from the other at this point of time.

We are out of the hostel with our bags packed by evening. Each one of us has a distinct destination. We bid each other goodbye before we embark on our respective journeys. We may have similar goals, but each one of us has to take a separate path to reach our goal. We walk together a few miles, but the rest of the journey is to be completed by us on our own. It is a matter of our choice to select people we can take along with us or bear the brunt of travelling alone.

I go to the bus stop. I am to travel to Dhule to my aunt's place. My cousin is getting engaged the next day and married on the day next to that of the engagement. My whole family has already reached there. I have reserved a seat two days prior for myself. It's a night travel of about eight to nine hours. I am seated in my seat, and there is a middle-aged man as my co-traveller, sharing the seat with me. They put off all the lights in the bus after around 10 p.m. The man next to me is deep asleep, or so he pretends to be. He leans on my side and puts his head on my shoulder. I have to wake him up and tell him to sit upright. I am wide awake, alarmed, and anxious. Why did I not listen to my father? He wanted to come and take me. Since it is a new route and I am to travel alone, he was worried. But overconfident that I am, I did not listen to him. After the same thing got repeated once or twice, I retreat to a corner of the seat and place my bag in between the two of us. Some time of the night passes by uneventfully.

At around 1 a.m., I feel someone touching my lower back from behind. When I turn around in the darkness, I see the two men sitting on the seat behind me fast asleep. I look around in the bus, people are snoring, nobody is alert, and there is total darkness. It is pitch black. I can hardly see my own hand in the darkness. I do not know what to do. I experience the same sensation once again. I have to do something about this, I decide, and I have to act fast. I remove a safety pin from my purse. At the next touch, I prick the safety pin very hard into the darkness near my back. I hear a small cry and then all is well. I guard myself from any more calamities for the rest of the night.

Touch is a very good tool to express love, friendship, companionship, or even a casual association. But when it comes to strangers, we Indians are very averse to it. A casual innocent touch is fine with most of us. Intentionally touching an unknown person at the wrong places is unwelcome. I want to see who that person is, and I decide to teach him a lesson at daybreak, but he gets down at 4.30 a.m., when the rest of the people are still asleep. I pray to God to put some sense into this man's head and forgive him for his wrongdoings. I have no other choice because unless and until I forgive him, the thought of a revenge and helplessness on my part would not leave me. I would lose my peace by getting angry at him and for my inability to react. I feel bad at having lost an opportunity to reform him. I am immature to undertake the task of restructuring or transforming a human being. Maybe I should take up psychiatry to achieve this. I reach Dhule and find my cousin standing at the bus stop to take me home. I am thrilled to see him so I hug him and have tears of joy in my eyes. What all women need to be treated with is dignity and respect.

CHAPTER EIGHT

We come back from the vacation after the declaration of our results. Most of us have done well. I have a distinction in physiology, the subject I like. Vidya has a distinction in anatomy and physiology. Smriti has done well in biochemistry. Amruta has managed to pass all the three subjects given her lack of concentration in studies. Simran has missed her distinction in anatomy by two marks and in physiology by three marks. Ragini, Poorvi, and Poonam score a first class in all the three subjects. We are happy to be back and sharing our holiday experiences with each other. Our class result has been 100 per cent. It's a record in many years of HP history. There is going to be no casual batch after us.

Our college and clinical postings begin in three days. It is a Friday, and Monday onwards our second MBBS starts. We complete the formalities of paying the fees and go to the hostel.

Vidya is going to her maternal uncle's place in Thane as she usually does, whenever there is a holiday.

'Why don't you come along with me? We will have a nice time along with my cousins.' She insists on me going with her.

'I am going to Dadar. You can come with me to my aunt's place. We can go for shopping from there,' Amruta says.

'Girls, you all go to your relative's places, I am fine here. I love being in the hostel. The only problem is the food on Sunday. As the mess is closed, I have to rely on the vada pav which is sold on the street outside our hostel gate. I do not feel like going out of the hostel for dinner alone,' I inform them.

'Why don't you call Raj and go for food with him?' Smriti questions me.

'I would have loved to, but that would give him some wrong signals. He still hopes I would someday be his girlfriend. He called me up thrice during this vacation and kept me informed with the happenings on campus.'

'I can do something about your dinner. I shall be back on Sunday evening, and we can go for dinner together.'

'Why do you want to miss the company of your family, Poonam? I shall mange to eat something.'

'As it is, I am leaving now, so I will get two whole days to spend with my sister and her family. I can definitely manage to come back.'

'Okay fine, come if possible.'

Everybody from my class does a vanishing act by evening. This has happened so many times previously, but I had my studies then. I have nothing to do at present. I go out in the evening to buy my second-year books. I am at the bookstore when my hair gets pulled from behind. I do not have long hair, it is just shoulder-length, so there is no chance of it getting entangled into something. I look behind to find Raj and Vishal standing there.

'What are you doing? Already started studying for the second year?' Vishal questions me.

'Everyone's gone to some relative or acquaintance staying in Mumbai. I have no one staying in Mumbai, whom I can visit. I have to do something to pass my time.' There is a tinge of sadness in what I say; how much ever I try to hide it, I cannot do it. 'I am really bored of being alone in the hostel every weekend. I have returned from home recently and am homesick.' I suddenly become aware of the fact that I have said the wrong words in front of these people. I cannot chew my words back.

'We are here to help you, dear. Why don't you come for dinner with us?' Raj asks me.

'I have to have dinner in the mess today since I have already given the coupon in the morning,' I blurt out without thinking. We actually have to give our coupons in the mess if we are to have dinner that evening. We have twenty free coupons in a month. They are not actually free but compulsory; we pay for them with our hostel fees.

'Good, we can go for a picnic tomorrow. We can start early in the morning.' It is difficult to dampen Raj's enthusiasm.

I stand there staring at the book in my hand, speechless. I have no alibi, and I am in a fix. I do not want to go out with this man, and I cannot find any reason not to. What do I do? My brain is running at a top speed, and I am still numb. My face gives away all my feelings. Raj speaks up again, 'You do not have to force yourself to come with us. I just thought we would show you the real Mumbai. It is up to you whether to come or not.'

'Raj, what do you mean by *we*? You two can go. Who else is going with you?' I am perplexed by Vishal's question.

'Vishal, you are also coming with us. Do you think she would trust me to go alone with her? Have you not seen her? How cautious she is? You can never catch her off guard.'

'It is not a question of trusting you, Raj. I am not a fun-loving person like you guys. You will be bored in my company.'

'Do not worry, we will not let you and us get jaded. I shall see you tomorrow morning at seven at your hostel gate.' They go away before I can say anything.

I wake up the next day to the loud knocking on my room door. It is Pooja. 'Shalinii, wake up. Raj is at the gate since half an hour waiting for you. I saw him and asked what he is here for, he would not reply. I asked him if he wants me to send you. He said, "Just see if she is awake, don't wake her up." Are you going someplace? Vishal is also with him.' Vishal, Raj, and Pooja are friends and know each other very well.

'He is taking me around to see places in Mumbai. I have been sort of pulled into this. I have nothing to do today, I accepted their invitation.'

'You do not have to give me an explanation. You will never get these days again, Shalinii. Make the most of them. Today being a Saturday, a half day for college, there is a movie in the MLT. It is fun to watch a movie in the MLT, so come back by 6 p.m. You did not enjoy your first year and you cannot enjoy your third year, have fun this year at least.' I wonder at what exactly Pooja wants to tell me. I got it that she wants me to enjoy the movie. I wonder if there is a warning of sorts in her words, a signal for me not to be late and return early. I am not fond of any parties or late-night shows. Anyways, that is not possible for the average

Mumbaikar, least of all a medical student. I trust Vishal and Raj. I have known them for more than a year. But *but* always comes in between. I have never been all alone out with boys ever. What would my friends say? What would my parents think if they know this?

I wake up slowly contemplating my next move. I see the two of them standing outside through my window. I have to hurry. I go to the bathroom and find there is no water supply. 'They have cleaned the overhead water tank,' informs the sweeper to me.

'What do I do now?' I murmur to myself. I go to my room and fetch my drinking water bottle. I brush my teeth with that water and wash my face. I change into nice, clean, ironed clothes, put on some perfume, and I am ready to move out. Raj is elated to see me. I can make it out from the big broad grin on his face.

'What exactly is the plan?' I ask audaciously, not letting them into my cynical world.

'We were under the impression that you would decide. We will take you wherever you desire,' Raj answers merrily.

'Is there any place you want to visit in particular?' Vishal asks me.

'No. I do not want to visit any specific place'. I inform them. I want to escape but I suppress the words, can I go then,' adding instead, 'I shall be your guest, you decide where to go.'

'Do you believe in God?' Raj asks me.

'Yes, I do,' I say.

'Let us begin by visiting a temple.'

I instantly agree. 'Which temple do we go to? I have already been to the famous Siddhivinayak temple.'

'You come with us, we will be your guide today.'

Raj is his usual self, joking and laughing all along. All my prejudices and fears of going with them evaporate in no time. The two of them treat me as if I am one of them. My gender does not seem to bother them or me either. There is no indecent behaviour on their part. In fact, they are very protective about me. We visit the Mahalakshmi temple. We sit on the rocks behind the temple and keep looking at the sea, each of us lost in an unknown world. We are together, but there is no communication for some time. We then visit the Haji Ali Dargah. The next is lunch at a hotel serving Gujarati Thali. We discuss nuclear power plants, NASA, our government, our college, the books we read, our families, our aims in life, our friends.

'We need to go back. There is a movie in the MLT at 6 p.m. today,' I inform the others after lunch. It is 4 p.m. by then.

'We can watch a movie in the MLT any other time. There is a movie there every month. It is our exam term, we would not be coming out like this again. You can watch a movie next time,' Raj reminds me about their exams. 'Have you ever been to a play,' he adds.

'You mean a Marathi play? No, I have never been to any play.' This is when I apprehend for the first time that the three of us speak Marathi.

'It's fun to watch a Marathi play, you will enjoy it. Of course you have to develop a liking for it. Let us go for some play,' says Raj. We are still at the hotel paying our bill which we share amongst ourselves. Raj gets the *Times of India* to check for a suitable play.

It is my first experience to watch a play. Raj has selected a comedy one, and I laugh more than what I have laughed in the entire one and a half years of my stay in Mumbai. I am introduced to a new world by these two friends. At times when I do not understand, I take the help of the two of them, and they enlighten me. The climax of the play is serious, and I start crying. I just cannot stop the tears flowing from my eyes. The two of them laugh at my childishness.

'Come on, Shalinii, it is no more than a play. It is not real. How can you cry?' Vishal says still laughing out loudly as we move out of the theatre. My eyes swell up immediately after I cry, and any Tom, Dick, and Harry can make out that I have been crying. I do not utter a single word on our journey back to the college. The two of them understand my need to be alone and leave me to deal with myself. They talk about their studies and plan how they would study in this term and prepare for the exams. I am listening to them, but a part of me is still stuck up with the play. I do not like the note on which the play ends. The two lovers in the play have a very carefree attitude towards life and love each other dearly. The female protagonist makes her love known to her lover. He does not express it to her even when she is at her deathbed due to cancer. I at last make my worry known to the others.

'People do not articulate themselves due to many reasons they consider valid. What do they achieve by doing that? Many a times we think in a particular direction, of a consequence, in a certain situation and reach a suitable conclusion, which never in reality occurs or happens. We are already there where we may never be. If it is a positive thought, mull over it, but if it is a negative one, there is no point in reflecting about it. We need to drop it and communicate to prevent confusion and uncertainty in the minds and lives of the people concerned in that matter.' My tone is serious beyond my own recognition when I say this.

'Is it not possible that he does not want to hurt her? Maybe he does not consider himself worthy of her love or he has some other barrier which he cannot overcome. Life is not a bed of flowers, it is like this play, Shalinii. You cannot always live life on your terms and conditions. There are rules in life that need to be followed. You cannot be a winner at all times. You do not get what you want most of the time and still life goes on. It does not wait for anybody. It is not about your likes and dislikes. I love you, you don't love me. I am fine with it. Someday you will like somebody and appreciate what I am saying. I will get married to some person whom I will develop a liking for. How we live our life is for us to decide. How we take failure in our stride and rejoice at our successes is our destiny.' I am amazed at Raj's maturity.

We are at my hostel gate. I bid the two of them goodbye and go inside. I go straight to the mess though I am not hungry. I want to finish the formality of eating food. I am tired and want to sleep early. I am still thinking of what Raj has said to me before leaving. Reshma, Raj's classmate is sitting in the mess. She says to me, 'Where have you been the whole day? You had gone for a movie, or did Raj take his princess around the city? You at all times deny that you are Raj's girlfriend and yet you go out with him.' There is poison in her dialect. I, on my part, am not in the capacity for an argument.

'Raj and I are good friends. What is the problem in me going out with him?' I counter-question her.

'A girl and a boy or a woman and a man cannot be friends. It is not possible for you to have a platonic relationship with a boy at this age. Why do you have to go out? You can be within the campus.'

I am already very angry, being troubled by the insensitivity of the male character of the play. I do not even feel the need to tell her that I was not alone with Raj. My friends are not with me today to talk to this girl. I feel helpless, and I have tears in my eyes. I go to my room and cry. Why am I crying? Is it because of what she said, or is it for some other reason? I ask myself. Have I essentially started liking Raj? I have no answer to it. He is a nice person, but it is as if I am trying to put him in a frame that is not made for him. There is Raj in front of me now and nobody else. I have not seen any other man this close. Maybe she was right. This is how people come together and fall in love. I feel as if I am convincing myself to like Raj. He is the one who has told me many times that he likes me. Am I happy for the attention he gives me? I am confused, and the more I try to tell myself all is well, the more I am lost.

I make another important decision: never go out with a boy or any person of the opposite sex alone. I can go in a group. However clear your heart, your intentions, or your conscience may be, there is going to be some interpretation by others. If you wish to flow against the tide, against the traditions, you have to be prepared to face the consequences. I sleep late, sometime in the early morning. I wake up at noon with a throbbing headache. I go to the mess after brushing my teeth. There is nobody there. I have lunch, and I go to bed again.

There is knocking on the door, I wake up with a jerk. There is Poonam standing at the door.

'You are sleeping at this hour? Are you not well? What is wrong with you? Do you have fever?' She showers me with questions.

'I am fine,' I say this, and I start crying aloud.

'What's the matter, Shalinii? Did something happen to you?' she asks tenderly.

I tell her all the events since the time she and the others left until the time she has come to my room.

'Shalinii, you should not get affected by what people say. Why did you not tell her Vishal was with you? She is jealous of you. She likes Raj, and she got an opportunity to trouble you unnecessarily. I will go to her room just now and make her feel sorry for what she did to you yesterday.' She is about to saunter out of the room when I stop her.

'Forget it, there is no point in talking to her. I should not have been emotional. I have been all alone and am feeling low, that's it. I will have a bath quickly, then we can go out for dinner.'

'Shalinii, go and tell Raj what she said to you.'

'No, Raj will be angry, and he might insult her in front of the whole class.'

'That is exactly what she deserves for poking her dirty nose in others' affairs.'

After our dinner is over, Poonam tells me, 'Shalinii, there is an STD phone near the blood bank. We can call our parents from there. Mandar informed me the other day. We require one rupee coins, many of them. I got them from my cousin today while coming. Let us go to call our parents.' I agree, and we go to the phone booth. There is a long queue there.

'Poonam, we will be late. Let us not wait. We will come some other day.'

'Shalinii, my father is not well. That is the reason why I want to call him up, people will finish fast. Nobody seems to be carrying many coins.'

I nod my head in the affirmative, and we stand in the queue. There are nearly fifteen people before us. But true to Poonam's predictions, none of them talk much. We are moving ahead rapidly. Poonam has the hopes of talking to her father soon. A postgraduate student enters the booth and removes out a bag full of coins. We look at each other and before we could talk him into letting us talk first, he starts talking.

'It looks like he is talking to his girl friend,' I say. Poonam winks her eye at me. We start discussing our schedules the next day onwards. This year we have our roll numbers according to the first alphabet of our surname. We forget the time and that man talks for almost an hour.

'Oh! God, Poonam!' I shout at full volume. 'It is 11.30. What do we do? The watchman will not open the gate. The keys would have gone to the warden.' I am loud enough for all the people in the queue to hear. I panic while Poonam tries to pacify me. The girl after us who looks like a postgraduate student says, 'Go and meet the CMO or AMO on duty. They will be able to help you.' We have not been to the hospital building. We ask her the directions to go to the CMO's office.

'Go straight and turn to the right, you will find the casualty, ask for the casualty medical officer (CMO). If you do not find him, go further down the lane where you will find the office of the assistant medical officer (AMO), meet him and narrate your problem to him,' she advises us.

We go and meet the CMO in the casualty and elucidate our predicament to him anxiously. 'Can you do something to open our hostel gate?' I ask him.

'The opening of the hostel gate is not in my hands. The warden decides that. If they open the gate once, everybody will demand opening it every day, and there would be no discipline. I can arrange for a place for you to sleep at night in the hospital. Go to the emergency ward and ask Pawan, the intern there, to open the side room of the major OT.'

I and Poonam go to the emergency ward. There is utter commotion in that ward. There are a variety of patients and many different doctors with a huge team of nurses. Nobody seems to be free. There is the wheezing sound of an asthmatic's breathing, vehicular accident patients writhing with pain. The medicine guys are busy reviving a cardiac arrest. The surgery people are shifting a blunt trauma with rupture of the spleen to the OT. The ENT residents, the postgraduate students, are busy doing a tracheostomy. There are two interns we could see, one of them is suturing a wound and the other is collecting blood. Whom do we approach in this pandemonium? We cannot stand this sight of absolute suffering anymore, and we are about to go out. At that instant, I spot the Blood Bank guy assisting in some procedure. I go and stand beside him to attract his attention. He looks up at me for a split second and then continues doing whatever he is doing without acknowledging my presence.

We go and stand in one corner and wait for him to finish his work. I keep looking at him once in a while to let him know that we seek his attention. He comes to where we are standing after half an hour.

'The eminent Shalinii comes to meet me in the casualty at such an hour. What an honour?'

'We want to meet Pawan, he is also an intern like you,' I say as fast as I could before he says something else.

'Why do you want to meet Pawan?' His voice drops to almost a whisper when he says that name.

I do not want to tell him the details. 'Some personal work, you see. Where can we find him?'

'I think he has gone to the surgical OT on the second floor, or if you don't find him there, check the male and female surgical wards on the ground floor.'

We go and rummage around all the places he has listed. Pawan is not to be found. We once again reach the emergency ward. The resident we had met in the OT has come to the emergency ward. He speaks to a guy with his head bent down, in reference to us.

'Pawan, these two have been looking for you. Somebody sent them to the OT.'

I am elated to have found Pawan at last. As Pawan looks up, I recognize him to be the Blood Bank guy, and I look at him with complete disbelief. He looks at me and smiles roguishly. He pulls my hand and gets me out of the ward in the passage outside; following close on my heels is Poonam.

'Don't look at me with those big eyes. I feel as if you are about to swallow me. Is it my fault that you did not know my name? Why do you want to meet me?'

'We were at the phone booth and got late, so our hostel door has been closed. The CMO told us to meet you and ask you—'

'Should I take you two to sleep in my room in the boys' hostel?'

'No. You are to open the major OT side room for us,' I screech aloud. A passer-by stops and asks me, 'Is there some problem, madam?'

'No,' I scream at him.

'Shalinii, relax, I am just joking. The surgery lecturer is sitting in the OT side room. Will you two sleep in the side room of the surgery ward? There is one bed, and it is not very big, enough for one person.'

'It is fine, we can adjust on one bed,' says Poonam.

Pawan opens the room for us. I and Poonam lie down on the bed. I cannot sleep in a new place, but I am very tired and go off to sleep in no time and so does Poonam. I am awakened by a slight noise, and I half open my eyes to see Pawan putting a clean white bed sheet from the ward over us. It has been cold, and I have been shivering. He walks out instantaneously. I am wide awake for the rest of the night, and we go to our rooms at six in the morning when the gate opens.

Chapter Nine

The clinical terms begin, and it is fun and a bit of stress too. Our daily schedule is very rigid. We are divided into batches. Each batch of students has to learn different medical subjects for a particular time period. We have lectures on the four second-year subjects whereas the clinical terms are of the third year subjects. The lectures start at 8 a.m. and continue up to 10 a.m. The wards or the OPD (outpatient department) or the OT (operation theatre), where we go next depends on the clinical posting that we have. The second-year lectures and practicals continue again from 2 p.m. to 5.30 p.m.

The clinical subjects that we need to study are surgery, medicine, gynaecology and obstetrics, and preventive and social medicine as the four major postings of three months each. The rest of the subjects like ear, nose, and throat medicine, ophthalmology, infectious diseases, orthopaedics, skin and venereal disease, psychiatry, and radiology extend between fifteen days to one month. We have four batches of fifty students. Each batch would be posted in one of the four major subjects and then rotate. All of us are together for all the second-year lectures. The subjects for practical are those of the second year. Here we are divided in separate batches of twenty-five students.

Simran, Poorvi and I are posted in surgery. There are six different units in surgery. Each unit has a unit head, professors, associate professors, lecturers, residents, and interns in a declining order of hierarchy, competency, authority and power. Fifty of us are divided in three and put in three units. The other three units of surgery have the third year students. One of the unit heads is the head of the Department of Surgery and is in charge and responsible for the proper functioning of the department. Similar is the structure in existence in all the departments. Each unit has an emergency duty once a week and on a Sunday once in every six weeks.

We reach the wards at 10.05 a.m. It is our OT day. We go on the second floor to the operation theatre and meet the lecturer there. It is our first experience in the OT. We are taught surgical hand washing. We become familiar with the atmosphere in the operation theatre. All of us are in a sombre form, and our faces are grim. People's life and death gets decided here. We fail to understand the attitude of the doctors in the OT that first day. How can these people be smiling, laughing, and cracking jokes we conjecture. The list of operations for the day is long.

I ask one of the junior residents, 'How long will the OT go on?'

'My name's Rajesh, and the OT will not be over before 5.30–6 p.m.'

'We have our lectures at 2.30 p.m.,' I inform him.

'You go for your lectures at that time, but the OT will continue.' This is his answer.

'When do you have lunch?' I am full of questions for people all the time. I have been a very enthusiastic person since childhood.

He has a nice nervous laugh at my question. 'We usually have a heavy breakfast before coming. Lunch is always after the OT gets over. The problem arises only when we do not get time for breakfast.'

'Why don't you wake up early and have breakfast? The canteen opens by 6.30 a.m.'

'Six days a week we sleep beyond 12.30 a.m. and wake up at 5.30 to 5.45 a.m. On the day of our emergency, even if we manage to sleep for four hours, we are lucky.'

'What do you keep doing whole day long?'

'You shall see. We do not come to know when days turn into weeks and months and months into a six-month term.'

'Do you like this life?'

'No,' he replies curtly and moves ahead with his work before I question him further.

The lecturer is operating on an appendix of a young girl. Two to three girls from my group collapse at the sight of the surgery and the blood. We support them, take them outside the OT and give them freshly prepared lime juice which is being served by the ward boy to all those present. The cold lime juice feels like bliss in this human mundane for the people present. I fail to recognize who is suffering more: the person getting operated or the one who is operating. This is the commencement of a long, never-ending journey to eliminate others' sufferings at the cost of what? The doctors are oblivious of their own needs in life. They have no time to reflect upon themselves.

We are made familiar with all the surgical instruments and the devices and gadgets used during and after the surgery. For each surgery, there is a team consisting of the operating surgeon, one or two assisting surgeons, and staff nurses. The other important person in the operation theatre on each table is the anaesthetist, one who puts the patient either to sleep or takes away the pain and other sensations from the body area to be operated upon. He is indispensable. All members of the team are crucial.

We attend our lectures and go to the canteen at 6 p.m. When we are leaving the canteen at 6.30 p.m., we see our surgery unit entering the canteen for lunch.

'Is it the end of today's work?' I ask Rajesh while washing hands at the basin.

'Not so early, the boss will take the post-operative rounds, and then I have to monitor the vitals of the operated patients. I have to take the evening rounds. Sujit, my senior who's called a registrar, will take rounds at night. He would confer certain orders, work to be done on some of the patients, and a final round at twelve midnight.'

I salute him and bid him a good bye.

I am attempting to identify and be on terms with the sort of life I have chosen. Being a student in a medical undergraduate school seems effortless to me at this juncture. This is in comparison to the postgraduates, who undergo a vigorous lifestyle worse than the armed forces recruits. No doubt people succumb to pressures. I have heard of students leaving and giving up their PG courses, developing friendship and comradeship to last a lifetime, at times committing suicides. I used to salute and have a reverence for the defence personnel; I contract an unusual awe for the Indian doctor.

It is our first emergency in surgery. We reach the wards after our lectures and snacks in the canteen in the evening at 6 p.m. We shuffle between the E-ward, which is the emergency ward, the minor OT, where minor procedures are done, to the major OT to the surgery male and female wards. We have one or two small clinics that is lectures in the side rooms of the wards by the lecturer or some PG student who manages to find some time off his agenda. By the time we have an awareness of the time in the clock and our stomachs are empty, it is past midnight. We have to go to a small hotel outside the hospital gate to have food. We are very hungry, so it tastes out of this world. We eat so fast that it gives an impression as if we have just returned from a famine-hit area.

After dinner, a few less-enthusiastic ones find a place to sleep and go off to sleep. The boys from the hostel go back to the hostel. We continue exploring the fun of the E-ward and make ourselves useful to the already exhausted residents by doing small tasks we can do, in the process learning the mysteries and exploring the depths of the surgical world. At 5 a.m., we are drained and weary.

Sujit, the registrar, sees us running around in a worn-out state. He says, 'What are you girls doing? You need to sleep now. Don't you have lectures and practicals tomorrow?' His words bring us back to our senses. We indeed have a complete working day plus a pharmacology viva we have forgotten about. We go to the side room and open our pharmacology book to read for the viva, and we fall asleep without our own knowledge. We wake up to hear the clatter around us, and the watch shows it to be 8 a.m.

'I am not attending the lecture we have at 8.30 a.m.,' Poorvi says. It is the lecture of the best professor in microbiology. I am fatigued and weary, but I do not have the heart to bunk it. I run to the hostel and wash my face, brush my teeth. There is no time for the formalities of changing my clothes or having a bath and eating something. I jog to the college to be late for the lecture by five minutes. My favourite teacher excuses me for it. But he questions me on my appearance. I am breathless and perspiring.

He asks me, 'Are you not well? You seem to be here just out of bed. Is something the matter? Do you want to go back?' There is laughter all over the classroom. I am too self-conscious to say anything. I just nod my head in the negative meaning I do not wish to go back. Mandar comes to salvage me by saying, 'She has been attending the surgery emergency the whole night and so is in this pathetic state right now.'

Before I could say a word, my teacher asks me, 'Did you have breakfast?' I again nod my head to signify no. 'Go and have your breakfast and come to me when you have time. I will teach you separately whatever I am teaching the class today. Bear in mind one thing, it will help you a long way in your life as a medico, do not ignore your breakfast. It is the most important meal of the day. We all have an overnight fast, so your blood sugars go low. Your digestive system is the most active in the morning after having rested the whole night. So breakfast is a must.'

I hear someone shouting, 'Special lecture for Shalinii, she is lucky.'

'Go to the canteen and eat.' I am happy. Poorvi will not miss the lecture now. She can attend it with me.

People in the medical college are caring. The dictionary meaning of *care* is what you experience from time to time. There is a healthy competition amongst students. Since each and every person shares the same experience some or the other time, it is recognition of you as me and me as you.

When we identify ourselves with another person, it is easy to carve our life without hesitation. There cannot be hidden agendas. There is a final, ultimate purpose which has to be attained by the entire community.

I love forensic medicine. It is amusing to study and read it. We have a viva in forensic and the questions asked are which road is your college on? What is the full form of BEST? These are fundamental general knowledge questions. The students are confounded and reflect the HOD to be out of his mind. 'He is trying to get information from us as he has recently shifted to Mumbai. He wants to increase his own knowledge.' These are the remarks passed by us. It takes us time to understand that our observations, knowing stuff around us, and general knowledge are the most significant aspects of forensic medicine. It also includes toxicology— the effect of toxins like the diverse venoms, the actions of various poisonous and non poisonous substances and drug abuse. We have to study in detail the identification of the types of poisonous and non-poisonous snakes, scorpions, their features, their effects, and treatment protocols.

Microbiology is the study of all aspects of microorganism with the study of the whole subject being done under the microscope. We learn about the culture mediums and preparation of the slides from body fluids and to check for the antibiotic sensitivity. We are taught how abuse of antibiotics can lead to development of resistant organisms which do not respond to routine medicines. It includes the study of the types of fungi, viruses, parasites, worms along with bacteria. The growth patterns of these organisms, their hosts, their staining qualities, their life cycle, transfer mediums which transfer them to us, their distinctive characteristics, diseases they cause, descriptions of similar diseases if seen in animals come within the confines of microbiology.

Pharmacology is the study of drugs that is medicines in detail. It includes the effects, the side effects, and the mechanism of action of drugs. The categories and groups of drugs, the interaction of drugs with other drugs or food, the safety of drugs during pregnancy and breastfeeding are portrayed in detail in our pharmacology books. The drugs that we use are studied thoroughly for their qualities and adverse effects, if taken in the normal doses and in excess, the antidotes of these drugs if any. There are certain medical treatment procedures other than the one we follow which are supposed to have no side effects, whereas the fact is the side effects have never been studied. Quality control is another important aspect in drug manufacturing. If these are not maintained, the drug may have disastrous effects rather than being curative. Presence of toxic trace elements like lead and mercury is a common occurrence in many non-allopathy medicines and alternative healing techniques. The cheap so-called generic medicines may not have been manufactured in stringent sterile environments and lack the efficacy to treat diseases as the drug may be less in quantity or poor in quality. If these generic medicines are used and the patient does not get well or his condition worsens, whose responsibility would that be? I wonder.

Pathology is the opposite of physiology. In physiology, we learn the normal functioning of the body organs and tissues. In pathology, we come to know what happens to these human cells, tissues, and organs in various functional derailments and during disease processes. It is a detailed study of alteration of the normal homeostasis of humans due to the effects of our surroundings. In conclusion, what is a disease? It is the body's response to any external abnormal stimulus. There is an age-old saying which goes 'A healthy mind in a healthy body'. This needs to be altered in today's scenario. It should go 'A healthy body in a healthy mind'. We have evolved to a stage where we are responsible for most of our ailments in this modern-day world.

The week passes off without our noticing it. It's about to be the weekend again, and I am in a foul state of affairs. It is Saturday afternoon, and the hostel will soon be empty. I hear Poorvi calling out my name on the mike installed on the ground floor of our hostel to call the girls down. I go down to find her and Ragini ready to go somewhere.

'Are you two leaving immediately?' I ask them.

'Yes, and so are you,' Ragini says this.

'I cannot come to your relative's place.'

'We are going to the college, and you are coming with us.'

I go with them without asking any further questions. They inform me on the way that we are going to a rock concert arranged by the cultural secretary in the college. I am not familiar with this kind of music. I know a few songs here and there. The event is rejuvenating and mind blowing. It leaves an everlasting impression on my mind. The singers who have been invited are professionals, and the music is lively. For the first time, I feel I have been missing on something so wonderful. I have tears of joy and sorrow, both during and by the end of the program.

As I return to the hostel, I find the lights in my room switched on. I have forgotten to put off the lights in a hurry I deduce. I reach my room to find the rest of my friends there.

'We have been waiting for you for dinner,' says Smriti.

'You have not gone home?' I question them.

'We have decided to spend this weekend with you.' It's Poonam giving her defence for not having gone home.

We go for a movie the next day after lunch. It is a newly released excellent one with the leading superstars in it. All of us are desperate to watch it and are disheartened and dispirited to find it to be houseful. Simran says, 'I will manage to get the tickets in black, just hold on and wait on one side.' Sure enough, she deals with the situation and gets the tickets at one and a half times the actual cost. When we enter the theatre, we find Anil, Mandar, and Sujay in the lobby.

'How did you get the tickets? Did you book them in advance?' I ask them.

'How did you get them?' This is the question asked by Mandar.

'We bought them in black,' I inform. All the three of them burst out into loud spells of laughter, and I cannot make out the reason. Anil explains me, 'We go to the manager and show our identity cards and tell him we are medical students and so do not get time to watch a movie, please give us tickets. They give us the tickets reserved for VIPs in the last row.' I feel bad for having unnecessarily paid more money. There is no point in brooding over what has happened, and I enter the theatre with a blissful face. We enjoy the movie and go out for dinner in a nearby restaurant. The three boys join us for dinner. We converse about the medical and surgical wards and the books to be bought and read for the diverse subjects of the second and third years of MBBS.

It is our turn to conduct the hostel day this year. We have to announce the hostel day and turn it into a reality.

The nine of us gather one day with three more additions. These are the girls staying in Panvel, which is far away, and everyday commuting is not possible for them. They managed to travel in the first year, but with onset of the clinical terms and the emergencies that we have to attend, it is not possible for them to travel daily. We fix the date and divide the work to be done by each member of our team. The management of any function requires the coordinated efforts of all its team members. The function is to be organized on the lawn of the hostel. The first and foremost thing is the finance required. We calculate the total expenditure and divide it by 80 per cent of the girls in the hostel. The remaining 20 per cent is for breakdown that is the expected in such tasks.

We start collecting money and make the payment for our part of the contribution immediately. The team arranging for the food goes to sample a variety of food at the restaurants within the vicinity of the hostel. The team accountable for the decoration and lighting moves out to meet the college electrician to make a list of the material required. The hostel day preparations are not less than an average Indian wedding. We plan vigilantly and execute the plan meticulously. I am made the team leader, and I lose my sleep for the last few days. I have nightmares wherein all the food goes stale or there is heavy rain in the month of December spoiling my show completely. We have arranged for a variety of games and dance performances along with a DJ and a music system. At times in my dreams, the DJ does not turn up or the music system does not work or there is lack of electric supply. I have not once experienced the power cut situation in Mumbai as in Nashik in the two years of my stay. But the anxiety and my perfectionism make me as if I am a patient of some obsessive compulsive disorder. My madness reaches an extent where on the last day before the event I am muttering in my sleep, 'Simran, are you sure the menu is perfect?' or 'Ragini, are the electricians coming on time or not?' Smriti wakes up with a startle on hearing my voice at 2 a.m. in a non-exam term. She shakes me, and I shout aloud, 'What? Things have all gone wrong.' She stirs me up and sprinkles a few drops of water on my face. When I am alert, she says, 'Shalinii, all is fine, sleep serenely. You are acting as if your daughter is getting married.'

The day of our testimony arises. Everything goes as per our plan, and we enjoy the evening very much. We are complimented by all present for our efforts to make it a memorable evening for them. The day is etched on our hearts forever and so is the bond between us. The hostel day is on a Saturday. I sleep the whole of the next day. It boosts a new confidence in me, and I have a heightened self esteem. If we can acknowledge ourselves well for our qualities and have a clear self-image, we appreciate others too. Unless we accept ourselves the way we are, we deny others an access into our world and do not attain the depths of their despair. We develop a distinctive way of celebrating our birthdays also. We buy cake the day before any of our birthdays and cut the cake at twelve in the midnight and then there is singing and dancing till the wee hours of the morning. We are developing an only one of its kind culture in the hostel and the college. We are unknowingly becoming the trendsetters, and we bask in the glory of our newfound happiness. We are undeniably emerging as champions of our very own lives at an early age and with a much faster pace.

CHAPTER TEN

I am in the postgraduate library one evening, hunting for a reference to a rare condition, an inguinal hernia in a female patient. This hernia is common in male patients; females rarely get it, and we have a patient in the ward with this condition. Raj is reading his pathology book and has two other path books open in front of him, and he is making notes. He is immersed in his work and does not see me. I go to say hello to him.

'Hi! Raj, how are you, and how is your exam preparation?'

'Oh! Shalinii, good you are here. I want to have a cup of coffee and did not want to go alone. I am bored as I am all alone in the room. I could not study there and have come to the library. Can you come with me to the canteen?'

'Where is your room-mate, Vishal?'

'Don't you know, Shalinii? He is admitted in the special room on the tenth floor. He has hospital-acquired infection.'

'I am not informed about the incidents in the hospital. I thought since it is your third term, you are busy preparing and hence are not seen around much. What is wrong with Vishal?'

'He will tell you himself. I should not be talking about it.'

'Is something serious? I mean is he recovering and admitted since when?'

'He has been in the ward for the past one week. He is recovering.'

'Why are you not telling me what is wrong with him?'

'He has contracted tuberculosis from the medicine ward. He collapsed one day in the room and became unconscious. Luckily, I was with him in the room. I immediately brought him to the casualty and admitted him. He is under the care of the chest physicians at present though he was initially in the ICU. He developed a pleural effusion along with a tuberculoma in the brain.'

'I do not get what you are talking completely. What I can make out is his lungs and brain are involved. I want to go and meet him.'

'He is in room number 1005 in the new hospital building. I came to the library after visiting him some time ago.'

I go to meet Vishal directly from the canteen, keeping my bag in the library. I knock softly at the slightly ajar door, out comes Pawan with a finger over his mouth signalling me to be silent. He closes the door behind me and says, 'He slept five minutes ago.' We hear Vishal calling Pawan in the room. Both of us enter the room. 'I have not slept, Pawan. Who is it?'

'It's me, Shalinii. How are you?'

'I am in good health, Shalinii, and living because of these two, Raj and Pawan. I am alive as an outcome of their hard work. One of them has been with me all the time these past few days.'

'Have you informed your parents that you are not well?'

'There is no need to entail them in his illness, he is doing well. They would unnecessarily be worried,' Pawan replies in place of Vishal.

'Shalinii, these two have not let me sense the deficiency of my parents. They have nursed me akin to a mother. What he says is factual, I am their solitary child. You have no clue about the myth contiguous to tuberculosis. For most people, it signifies death. People deem it analogous to cancer. My parents would die a premature death with anxiety.'

I do not talk to Pawan. He is pressing Vishal's feet. I leave in about half an hour. I am saddened by Vishal's illness. It becomes habitual for me to meet him once or twice in a day till the time he is in the hospital. He is discharged in about a week and is back to his studies. He wants to appear for the second-year exams.

It is a fact that we as medical students are exposed to a variety of infections. Most of the time, we contract a subclinical infection, which acts as a shield for us. Vaccines given to children, during childhood, work on the same theory. The diminutive infection induced incurs an immune response and activates the body's defence mechanism into action. This remains as a memory within the body, and the next time the same microbe hits the body, it is ready with its arms and ammunition, the various kinds of cells which destroy the microbe. But sometimes when the body's immunity is weak due to dietary deficiencies or stress or lack of sleep, the cells work as weak soldiers allowing the infection to set in, and we get symptoms. The initial symptoms act as a warning sign which if neglected, the militia of the microbes wins over the body cell mercenaries leading a person on to a copious illness entailing rest and medication. If missed at this time, the disease complex fully expresses itself, jeopardizing the person's routine body functions manifesting as generalized weakness, decreased appetite, body ache, fever, malaise, lack of energy and vitality. The next step is threat to life.

Health is not wealth in today's times. Wealth stands above all. The origin of 90 per cent of the illnesses is as a result of disregard on the part of the person suffering from the illness. As with any material thing, the body and the spirit demand care and maintenance. We service our vehicles, washing machines, televisions, telephones, computers regularly but not our own body as we do not buy it at a high cost in the market. It goes for repairing when it is completely non-functional, and then the blame is on the spouses, doctors, bosses, and so many other people. It is feasible to amend our immune system with a very positive attitude towards life. Genes, the basic units of humans, causing hereditary diseases such as diabetes can be altered with exercises of the mind and the body.

We consider God knows and does all the things and runs our lives. We and God are one is another belief. Where is God, and who is God? God is faith; God is power. We seek temples, churches, mosques in search of God. God is within us, within our inner selves. A disharmony within us is at the root of any illness. The body homeostasis alters with the discord between a person and his self, his inner voice, his soul.

I am deep asleep, and I wake up at 4 a.m. I have been dreaming about something. I feel as if I have not slept, as if my brain has been working actively in the night. Nevertheless, I am as fresh as a newly bloomed flower. I have committed to my memory every detail of the dream. I am wide awake, and the dream has shaken me to the core. I go all over my dream. I am sitting in a classroom and am taking music lessons. I am in a college which teaches nothing other than music. I am wearing a long flowery skirt and a sort of designer top with a hat and a belt over the top. I have not met or seen any of those classmates, and we are speaking a language distinct from the one I know. The only person I know in the classroom is Pawan. He looks not the same as he looks now; I know it's him. I retain information about my teacher as well. He is a handsome male, tall with good features, and distinct from the rest of us. I could draw a sketch of this man. I get a feeling as if I am in China, Japan, no, it is Taiwan in the 1920s. Was it a dream or a past life? I am at a loss to make out. I want to go to the library and check it out the first thing in the morning. I all of a sudden become interested in Taiwanese history. Am I trying to trace a connection between me and Pawan?

Geography is a subject I have failed to understand all through my school life. I used to mug up geography then and vomit it out in the exams. I had no clue where in the world China or Japan existed and what was their connection with Taiwan. I know not of the year 1920; I was born in the 1970s. I go to the library to check where Taiwan exists, to note that our college library has no other books than medical books. 'Where can I find books on history and geography?' I ask the librarian.

'Madam, you will have to go to some arts, science, and commerce college or the library in the university campus at Kalina or the BCL.'

'What and where is BCL, and where is Kalina?'

'British Council Library, it is in south Mumbai, and Kalina is between Kurla and Santacruz.'

'Thank you.' I thank him and give up the idea of going into the details of my dream.

I am not fascinated by the way I look in the dream. I have a very fair complexion as opposed to the dark, dusky, wheatish skin tone I have at present. I am no princess from the fairy tale, nor a central character from a book or movie. I am not the typical MB lead star either. I am what I am and am proud to be the way I am. I do not seem to have my present complexion. I am, however, not willing to label myself as ugly or not beautiful. If your skin colour is not white, does not mean you are not fine looking, attractive, stunning, striking, and gorgeous. You can be all this without being fair skinned.

Beauty is skin-deep, they say. I say beauty is much more than the skin. Is being beautiful on the outside a virtue? It could be similar to a boon in disguise. In India, people have an obsession for the fair skin colour. There is discrimination between children of the same mother on the basis of their skin colour. The fairer child has an advantage even in school. The first thing that is asked after a child is born is 'What is it? A boy or a girl?' as if the gender makes the child belong less to its parents. The next thing that the family wants to know is the colour of the newborn baby. All newborns are sweet, cute, and beautiful. The first question I would ask would be, is the baby healthy and fine? But again, health is not important to most of the people. Our population has increased to such an alarming level that the health of a person is not taken into consideration at all. For a country obsessed with money, we value designer clothes, travel by air, eat at fancy restaurants, need a vehicle of our own, but want health-care facilities to be cheap. We do not mind even if sterilization techniques are not followed, if the cost of treatment is less. We still want to boil and autoclave and reuse disposables and are happy to get concession for it. IV fluid bottles are recycled to make bottles for mineral water. Maybe the high temperatures that they are subjected to would kill the microorganisms, but what about its biohazards during storage and transportation?

Our surgery term ends, and we are now into medicine. We are learning in detail about asthma, tuberculosis, hypertension, diabetes, and so many other illnesses. We have case presentations and discussions on these illnesses. We seem to have no time to spare. It is interesting; time is less and a long way to go for all of us. It is a non-ending process of consuming knowledge. We the enlightened souls would then go on a rampage to utilize this stored memory for the betterment of our fellow citizens.

We attend overnight emergencies in this term also. We do not have to go to the OT. On a post-emergency day, there would be blood collections of more than a hundred patients in each ward. I would come to assist the interns and residents for it. I have learnt the art of collecting blood. I collect the blood of an old sweet lady in her seventies. Sakhubai is her name. She is admitted for drug resistant tuberculosis also known as MDR (multidrug resistant) TB. It is a condition in which the routine drugs do not act on the tubercle bacilli. The prognosis of these patients may be bad. Whenever I go to the wards, she would call me and greet me. She has two sons who hardly come to visit her. She is from a village in Vidarbha area of Maharashtra.

'Be careful, Shalinii, it is MDR,' the lecturer Dr Kulkarni warns me.

On the fifth day of her admission, Sakhubai asks me, 'How are my reports today?'

I am not aware of the investigations done on her, so I tell her, 'I shall verify them and tell you.'

I go and check her papers. The reports of the blood tests done on the first day of her admission are attached in her file but no fresh reports. I go back to her bed and ask her, 'Sakhubai, have they collected your blood today?'

'Yes, today morning,' she shows me the site from where blood collection has been done. 'The sister gave me a red injection as well which looked similar to blood.'

'What injection could be similar to blood?' I ask the resident there.

She says, 'None of the injections we are giving Sakhubai resemble blood.'

'Is it Rifampicin? I have read it gives a red colour to body fluids,' I question her.

'Rifampicin is not available in injectable form. It is an oral tablet,' she informs me, and I become aware of the limitations I have as a second-year student.

I then approach the sisters, the staff nurses whom we lovingly call staffy, for an explanation to Sakhubai's predicament. 'She must be daydreaming. We have not collected her blood,' Sister Surekha tells me.

'She has a small white sticking tape put there,' I maintain.

'Dear doctor, when the sisters are saying they have not collected blood, that means they have not. Why don't you ask the residents? We know the system well, you all come and go. I am here since your bosses were students.' This is the matron in her ear-splitting unambiguous voice. A resident from some unit is working in the ward. She waves her hand gesticulating me to go out of the ward. I capture the signal and move out of the ward, promising myself to return in the evening when the matron would not be there. Nobody challenges the matron. Hers is the last word as she is in charge of the ward.

My pharmacology practical continues long, and there is a tutorial announced for the next day, I have to study for it. I do not find time to go to Sakhubai. The next day, I again probe with the residents and talk to Sakhubai without the knowledge of the matron. There are no fresh reports on her paper. The treatment that she is receiving continues, and she improves to a certain extent to be discharged after a few days. I forget about the incident and am busy preparing for my first-term exams.

I return to the hostel one day to find most of the girls gathered in the TV room, and there is tumult there. I find Poorvi standing there and ask her, 'What is this about?'

She replies, 'Shikha, a third-year student, has hanged herself from the ceiling fan and is no more now. Her parents have been informed, and the body has been sent to the pathology and forensic departments for a post-mortem.'

'I have seen this girl in the mess at times. Isn't she the quiet and shy girl who used to be engrossed in her studies?' I ask.

Pooja is from her class; she says, 'She had few friends and would talk less. She had taken admission from a reserved quota but did not like it. She was an intelligent and a deserving student. She had scored well in her twelfth standard and wanted to take admission through open merit, but her parents felt it would facilitate and aid her during the postgraduate admissions. She was not in favour of reservations on the basis of one's caste. She believed it was a mode of discriminating her from the rest of us. We tried to incorporate her within us, but she had a low self esteem, as if she did not belong here. Many of us did not even know about her reservation quota admission. It was so ingrained in her mind that she would herself inform all of us and see our response. Medical students do not treat another fellow student as anything other than a colleague and friend.'

The suicide note found on her person says, 'I am solely responsible for my death and nobody else is to be blamed. I could not cope up with the life in a hospital and cannot see people suffering. I am incapable of studying the vast portion of the third year, and I do not want to fail. If I fail in the third year, people would feel I did not deserve to be here and got into medicine just because I got admission easily.'

What a psyche? She had been so disturbed and none of us had any inkling of it. She gave up her life unnecessarily. Such a messed up thinking she had! It made no sense to us, but it had been very important to her. We regret for not having known this before. We could have brainwashed her away from her skewed thought process. It is too late now. Each one of us has our studies to deal with; nobody has time to see what others feel or do. None of us would prod in others' affairs. We had taken it for granted that she wanted to study and score well which she always did. The girls, who have seen her hanging and have been close to her, have to go in for counselling to the psychiatry department. They could not function normally for days after her death. The incidence sent shivers down our spine, and we get closer to each other. Loneliness and withdrawal from the surroundings gives a person a distorted view of life.

Days are turning into months; time is flying at a great pace. I am in the male general ward on an emergency, watching a procedure called ascitic fluid tapping. Patient is Pandurang from Ratnagiri district. He has been a chronic alcoholic all his life. He is thin, malnourished, with a pot belly. His abdomen has bloated, mimicking that of a pregnant lady.

'He has liver cell damage. We will be removing this fluid by putting a needle in his abdomen,' the med registrar Yogesh explains to us. Pandurang's abdominal fluid is being tapped several times. His blood investigations are repeated every other day. I keep following up Pandurang's case each day. One day, I go to check his reports, but there are no reports. The white sticking tape put after blood collection is there on his arm. He gives a similar history as Sakhubai: some sister gave an injection resembling blood through his IV site and then collected blood from the other arm. It is strange, but the facts remain the same. Neither the staff in the ward nor the residents have an explanation for this. Both the patients were critical, old, with low chances of complete recovery, as good as terminal.

My sixth sense tells me something is amiss. I talk to a few senior girls from the hostel to understand the apt functioning of the wards in case I am missing on something. Someone might be injecting and giving certain drugs and collecting blood for some clinical trial. I am told none of the clinical trials in this hospital are secretive. They are official, and the ward staff has absolute information about it. I have confidence in both my patients that they are not untruthful. Though from a rural background, both are intelligent beings. Pandurang's condition worsens, and he goes into a hepatic coma in a day or two. Is my brain ringing a false alarm? How do I come to a truthful conclusion? I cannot sleep or concentrate on my studies. I want to talk to someone. I do not want to unnecessarily trouble my friends from the hostel. I want to investigate alone. I am anxious. What if it turns out to be dreadful? I have to be cautious. Where and how do I start? I am no detective, an Aquarian by birth. Aquarians are supposed to be born detectives. I want to confide in somebody. I do not understand whom.

In the hostel nothing remains private. Girls cannot digest secrets. If I tell one person, it is bound to reach at least three others in one day. Boys are better in this respect. I am facing a dilemma. I am not close to any guy whom I can divulge my fears to. I think of Raj. No, not Raj; he has his second-year exams. It has to be a guy from the non-exam going terms and one who is relatively free from the load of exams. I keep thinking all the time. I dream of a boy rescuing me from the clutches of death one day. I am becoming insane over an issue which may not exist.

CHAPTER ELEVEN

I am sitting with my friends one Saturday afternoon for lunch in the canteen. I eat in the canteen and stay the whole day in the college and library as I cannot read a word in my room. I change the order I give to the waiter thrice and at the end of it sit stirring my food not able to eat much of it. I am not a part of the conversation and jokes my friends are sharing at the lunch table. All of a sudden, Pawan as always appears out of nowhere. 'Excuse me, girls, I want to talk to Shalinii.' I hear the voice but do not respond as if I do not know what to say to him. I hear Vidya say, 'You are excused, and you can talk to her, we have finished our lunch and are off to the hostel.' Pawan sits across the table as the girls get up, bid me goodbye, and move towards the canteen door. I drop the spoon from my hand and look up at him. He holds both my hands and literally shakes me up.

'Shalinii, what is the matter with you? Are you not well? I have been observing you since the past few days. I do not want to trouble you. I could not pass by when I saw you today. You have lost some weight as well. What is the matter?' There is anguish in his voice. He is looking directly into my eyes, and whatever he communicates at that moment through his gesture, I burst out and start crying aloud. He is astounded and so are all those sitting around us. He is not embarrassed, I notice. He comes across, sits beside me, and consoles me. I hide my face in my palms. He offers me water to drink. I gulp down the whole glass. He does not ask me what it is that I am crying for. He holds me by my hand and leads me to the MLT. The movie is about to start, and we sit to watch it without saying a word to each other.

I have heard the students of HP describing how it is to watch a movie in the MLT. My personal occurrence confirms what they meant. You are not watching a movie alone. It comes as a package deal of countless comments. It is analogous to having extra spice on an already luscious meal or your favourite topping on a delectable ice cream. Some things are beyond depiction. You have to experience it sitting there for those three hours. My vocabulary stretches out and takes a huge leap in those few hours. Pawan's presence has been an added asset at that time; otherwise, I would never have understood what has been going on. I am not asking him any questions. He is giving me a running commentary of the drama unfolding in front of us. I feel like a small child watching a cricket or a tennis match for the first time. The words I am introduced to are not from my daily dialect. I am in a shadowy, sinister world, I am learning to enjoy being a part of it. It is a medical college where nothing human can be hidden. It's an open milieu with no gender bias. I say goodbye to Pawan, come back to my room immediately after the movie.

When a person is lonely and has a perceived problem, a sweet talk is enough to soothe an anxious mind. Pawan plays that role for me at present. We are sharing an attachment ahead of spoken words. The further I trace the connections in my memory, he has always been there since a long time. The picture which had been ambiguous to me for years is clearing. Whenever I have had problems in my life since childhood, I have visualized Pawan with me. The image was vague then. Am I envisioning the non-existent? Why do I sense a familiarity to him? I spend the night half asleep, half awake with these and similar thoughts and dreams. There is no one from my group in the hostel. I have a lazy Sunday and am late for lunch at the mess. I am hungry, not having eaten the night before. I go to Swad, to find Pawan sitting there alone. Is this a coincidence? I want to dissuade myself from thinking otherwise.

'Hi! Pawan!'

'Hi! Shalinii, you look fine today.'

'Yes, yesterday's movie did wonders to me.'

'You want to give the credit to the movie?'

'No, actually I should be thanking you.'

'No need to do that, tell me, what's wrong?'

'How did you guess that there is something wrong?'

'You have a bad habit of counter-questioning others, why don't you answer straight away?'

'Well, have you ordered your food? I am starving.' I hide into the menu card.

'No, I have not had the time to order, you followed me before I was seated.'

'You mean I followed you?'

'Come on, Shalinii, you are making a mountain out of a molehill. We came here each independently without the knowledge of the other, it is no coincidence. I mean we are here because God wants you to get out of whatever it is that you are holding on to. What is on your mind, tell me all about it without being superficial.'

'Pawan, I have seen two very sick patients in the male and female wards complaining of being injected with a blood-like thing and whose blood collection had been done without the staff or the resident's knowledge. What it is I do not have the slightest idea, but it is bothering me. I smell something fishy.'

Pawan first laughs. 'I thought it is about your personal life.' Then on a more serious note, he adds, 'Now that you mention it, I recall a similar incident I faced a few days ago in the surgery ward. There was a patient of a vehicular accident in his fifties with multiple fractures and head injury. He was critical, not conscious, but his wife said precisely identical words. We did not trust her and thought she had a delusion due to sleepless nights at the hospital besides her husband.

'Shalinii, you amaze me. I have been wondering what it is that you are going through. I thought you had a setback at home or a hitch in the hostel or a failed love affair. You have been troubling yourself for this. Agreed, it is a grave crisis and we will have to find out what it is, nonetheless, bothering oneself so much over it seems unnecessary.'

'I appreciate what you are saying, Pawan, but that is the way I have always been.'

We notice the waiter waiting for us to give our order. 'A club sandwich for me,' both of us say at the same time. The waiter looks from me to Pawan who summarizes it for him, 'Two club sandwiches with two cups of tea.'

'I did not say tea, why did you ask one for me?'

'Shalinii, don't tell me you do not want tea. A club sandwich with tea is refreshing for me.'

'Me too, I was just pulling your leg,' I say with a naughty grin. I have shared my secret, and I feel free. Pawan has not wronged me or denied whatever I told him. He has shared a similar episode and not made a fool out of me. I am happy in the company of this man. Pawan jokes about the hairstyle of a woman sitting behind me, and our laughter fills the air around us. At that moment, Vishal and Raj enter the restaurant. Both of them are flabbergasted to find us together.

'You did not mention Shalinii was waiting for you and so you moved ahead of us, Pawan.' Raj tries to make it a lighter moment with a smirk. His facial expressions give away his displeasure.

'Raj, I was very hungry as I told you a while ago, I came ahead. She followed me. I had no idea I would meet her here.' Pawan's justification does not sound convincing to Raj.

'I did not follow anybody! Our mess closed by the time I woke up so I was forced to come here for lunch. I found him sitting alone and joined him.'

The waiter brings our food. The sandwiches are ready earlier than other times.

'Is nothing else available to eat? I hate to eat a sandwich for lunch,' Raj says this.

'Both of us love these and so are eating it, you can order your favourite masala dosa, Raj,' Pawan says.

'Both of you seem to know too much about each other's likes and dislikes, is it not?' Raj's tone is venomous.

'Raj, let me clarify, there is no question of me knowing her likes and dislikes. I met her here just now. Do not misunderstand us,' Pawan says coolly

'Oh really, did you not hug her in the canteen yesterday when she was crying? Then you took her to the MLT holding her hand, and you watched the movie sitting on each other's lap. How could you do that, Pawan? I may be studying in my room, but I keep a tab on whatever happens in the college.' Raj's words come as a thunderbolt on our ears.

'Raj, you have got the wrong information from whoever told you that. Shalinii was crying, and I consoled her. We saw the movie together, the rest is untrue.' Pawan is as cool as ice. 'She was in need of some companionship, I was free.'

'You do not need to give her company, you should have sent me a message, I would have come down,' Raj says this accusingly as if Pawan has committed a crime.

Pawan loses his cool. 'Why should I inform you? I saw her in trouble and helped her.' He calms down immediately. 'You have your exams, and I thought it unwise to disturb you.'

'Nothing in this world has more value for me than her, not even my exams.'

'Listen, both of you, you are very good friends of mine and full stop. I respect and like the two of you but I am not a commodity belonging to either of you. Do you think females are something to be possessed and decorated on your sleeves? If you truly love me, Raj, as you claim, let me be the way I am. I have not done anything that would put me to shame or would not fit in the Indian moral values that all of us have grown with. I love my independence and cannot live to rear children or serve my spouse or in-laws. I have my own individuality and thinking capacity, and I cannot give it up. I am a rebel and rebels have no place in the society, they are either outlaws or kings. I cannot predict today which way my future is. I am not willing to carry anybody into an indefinite space. If you want to be my friends, forget this talk ever happened and do not create bad feelings for each other over me.

'Order your food, Raj and Vishal, and share the sandwiches till then.' I talk sternly at first, dropping to a lovable tone later on.

'You sound like my mother,' Pawan says sadly staring blankly.

We munch at the sandwiches mutely. The waiter gets feedback forms to be filled. Raj and Vishal are eating their food hurriedly on its arrival. I and Pawan remove our pens to fill the forms. We have the same pens; all of us notice and smile at each other. It's a day of too many coincidences.

Before we go our ways, Vishal says, 'It's nice to be acquainted with you, Shalinii.'

'Same here, Vishal. Bye and all the best to both of you for your exams.'

I reach my room back and am trying to put some light at the way human beings function. How the context changes the outlook of each human being. Raj and Pawan, two good friends who have shared a lot of time of their lives together, doubt each other's intentions at the slightest provocation. Each would be willing to lay down his life for the other. They would not hesitate to hit out at some third person if the situation demands. Will their friendship stand the test of time when their individual interests are at stake?

What is life? Is it our thoughts, our perspective of looking at things, our day-to-day activities, friendship, love, hate for folks or communities, feelings for ourselves? What does a man strive for? Happiness and where is happiness? I am yet to find a person who is happy at all times. There is happiness in the eyes of a two-year-old when he sees his mom after being away from her for just some time. The same person outgrows his mother's height and then cannot smile at her even if he wants to. We, at a given time, are the refined product of the circumstances, state of affairs that we come across until that moment. It is not possible for us to be free of the bonds we strap ourselves with during our journey. We avoid and resist things, people, situations, and places, to gain what? We want to keep us from experiencing a bad feeling for ourselves. Who decides what is good and what is bad? We have heard it from elders and people around us. This is the hearsay evidence, and it has no significance even in a court of law. We let ourselves be guided by the age-old principles without knowing the details when those choices, conclusions, and resolutions were made, and we simply follow. Life has a simple principle: be happy in the conditions that you are in and make efforts smilingly to reach where you want to, not at the cost of others.

Eachday seems to be filled with new challenges for me, and I enjoy it. As I am leaving the hostel the next day for my morning lecture, Raj approaches me. In my zeal to reach the classroom on time, I do not notice him until he is right beside me, and he calls out my name.

'Shalinii, Shalinii, listen.'

'Yes, Raj, what is it?' I am sort of jogging as I talk to him, and he too jogs to match my pace.

'Shalinii, I want to apologize for yesterday and talk to you about something else as well.'

'Can you meet me in the canteen at two today? We can have lunch and talk.'

'That would be fine with me.'

I enter the classroom just before our microbiology teacher. He is talking about viruses, and my mind wanders as to what it is that Raj wants to talk to me about so urgently.

His prelims are beginning in a week's time. What am I to do if he proposes me directly? I do not want anything to come in the way of his career. I do not like microbio and the microscope. It all seems very boring to me. I am lost in thoughts, and Mr Nair, our teacher, is asking me the characteristics of the coxsackievirus. I come back into the present after being shaken by Vidya who is sitting beside me. It takes me a while to realize the question. Luckily, I have read the virus, and I start with 'There are two types of these viruses, group A and group B', and I give a brief description of each of the groups.

Mr Nair is perplexed. I tell him whatever he had said a few moments ago. 'Were you awake or asleep or somewhere in between?'

I tell him the truth. 'Sir, I was lost in thought, but I was also listening to you. I was not sleeping for sure. I had read this yesterday, and so it was a revision for me when you were teaching. I shall be present in the class henceforth. I am sorry, sir.'

'It's a rare quality women possess. They can be at many places at the same time. The neurons in their brain are tuned to multitasking. It is the same phenomenon in the female species of many mammals.' Our dear Nair sir forgot the virus and went on to the female species. He had wanted to be a psychiatrist but landed up as a teacher of micro. He had not been admitted to a medical college. He completed his master's and then a doctorate in microbiology from a prestigious college in the UK and came back to join a medical college to be associated with medical education. He is a keen observer of people.

'Microbio is not a difficult subject. You do not seem to be here, Miss Shalinii. I have seen you before during my lectures. Today you are physically present in the classroom. Do you have some exams?'

'I was completing my pathology journal late yesterday night.' I have to tell lies. I lied would be more accurate. Nobody has forced me to be dishonest. He has not asked for an elucidation. I want to prove that I am such a nice person or it is not my mistake. If we do not want to confront the truth, it does not mean we embark on falsehood. I could have said, 'Sir, I do not have any exams. I could not concentrate in the class as I have something else on my mind.' By saying this, my impression would have been appalling in front of my teacher. Why are we so obsessed with what people think about us? We are willing to do anything to remain in others' good books. In the process, we lose ourselves and forget who we are and why we exist. People are very judgmental about themselves and others. Their life is about who did what, when, how, why. They never stop asking questions to themselves and others. It is good to be curious, not to the extent that it becomes a headache for ourselves and those around us.

It is the beginning of my next lecture, and I get a nauseated feeling owing to the lack of sleep and hyperacidity for having skipped my breakfast and of course the ever-expanding thought process. I cannot sit for the lecture. It is the first time I am going to miss some lecture. I feel dreadful about it, but health matters most. I have to run to the ladies common room the next moment, and I vomit out sticky acidic fluid. I keep getting severe bouts of vomiting until I get bitter greenish bile out. Some girls have their glances on me, and they do not look normal to me. A postgraduate girl not known to me asks me if I am fine or not. I have a severe headache, and I run to the canteen to eat something. I order a medu vada, but the sight of it gives me nausea again. I finally have bottled cold sweet milk which helps me stabilize for some time. I go to the library and sit in a chair and put my head down on the table. I sleep instantly in the soothing effect of the air conditioner. I have a dream in which I am falling off a mountain cliff into a deep valley. I wake up to see that my head has been falling off the table. I readjust my position and am asleep in no time again. I wake up to find Raj whispering my name in my ears so as to wake me up. I look at him blankly without giving any input to my brain. Vidya, who's been tracking me, arrives. Taking a clue from Raj's actions, she holds my arm and both of them jointly manage to make me stand on my legs. I still have a vacant stare and am conscious as they try to make me walk. The sleep has done me some good, and my headache is less and I feel better. Together we move out of the library. We begin to talk as soon as we move out.

'Why did you sleep here? Are you unwell?' Vidya is the first one to break the silence.

'I have been looking for you all around since more than an hour.' This is Raj.

'What is the time?' I ask. Glancing at my watch, I say, 'Oh! It is four thirty. I have missed all my classes today.'

'It's okay if you do not attend classes for once. Do you want to have lunch? We will have to go out of the campus. Lunch would not be served in the canteen at this time,' Vidya says this.

'Did you finish your lunch, Raj?' I question.

'No, are we not supposed to eat together?'

'Vidya, Raj and I will be eating at Milan's across the road, you can carry on with whatever you are doing. I shall see you at the hostel by seven in the evening.' I know if Vidya is with us, Raj would not open his mouth to talk whatever he wants to express. He has his exams, and I do not want him to squander his time more than what he has already done. Vidya and I are on such terms at present that she would understand what I am saying. I do not need to clarify anything to her. She waves me a quick goodbye and turns around and walks in the opposite direction.

Relationships should be like this, transparent to the core. Friends and acquaintances become apprehensive if we lead an inauthentic way of life. It does not carry us long. We falter early in life. Vidya is sure it is something important that Raj and I want to talk, and she knows I will go and tell her whatever it is as soon as I get back to the hostel. This confidence is what Vidya has developed for me over time. Here both Vidya and I are important. We have created a space for each other where each has respect, love, and faith in the other. I have made myself worthy of her reliance, and she is not cynical.

We are seated in the restaurant. Raj is lost in thought; maybe he is mulling over how to begin talking whatever he has in mind. I wait for him to begin the conversation. Being impatient, I ask him, 'What is it that you want to talk to me about, Raj?'

'Shalinii, I want you to be happy in life. You can choose to be with Pawan if you like him. I do not want you to hesitate because of me. I do not want you to contemplate over your decisions as a result of my feelings for you.' While he is saying all this to me, the sadness on his face and in his tone is not hidden from me.

'Raj, you do not have to think so much. Concentrate on your studies. I like Pawan as much as I like you. I have not imagined myself in a relationship with anybody to this date. There is something else that I wanted to talk to you since a very long time. I see an opportunity to tell you about it today. I accept you love me a lot. What does that mean to you, Raj?'

'It means the world to me, Shalinii. I think of you most of the time.'

'Exactly, you have put me on the throne of your kingdom and made me your queen. I am a normal human being like any other person. Why me?'

'Shalinii, that is because you are loving and caring. You do not hurt a soul. You are truthful, and you live life on your own terms and conditions. You have a childlike innocence and simplicity.'

'Yes, Raj, but I am not the perfect human being, nobody is. I have some other faults. Each person is an amalgam of good and bad qualities. Why is it that you love one and not the other? You saw and met me at a juncture in your life when you were in need of a companion. You presumed that I am the best for you, which may not be true. You then held me in high esteem, your thoughts revolved around me and that is how you fell in love with me. The biggest myth in humans is that we fall in love, and it happens on its own. It is an intelligent choice that our mind makes according to the data that has been fed into it over the years. The other myth is that we fall in love only once. We are capable of falling in love over and over, again and again with every human being we meet. To avoid chaos in the society, we have the system of marriage. We abide by this system. It is the greatest structure that exists in our society. I salute the person who brought it into being. Faithfulness, loyalty, having sex with one partner, is our unsurpassed spirit. I do not agree that we fall in love accidentally.'

'Why are you telling me all this, Shalinii?'

'To make you aware of the fact that you are capable of falling in love with anybody on this earth as much as with me. Secondly, you can be with a person whatever way he or she is, if you really want to be with him or her.'

'I fail to understand your second statement, Shalinii.'

'Have you heard of people getting divorced? The rate of divorces around the globe is going up. I am making two contradictory statements both with meaning and value. We are capable of falling in love with everything every minute of our presence on the earth. At the same time, we are capable of being loyal and faithful to one person all our life if we so decide and desire in spite of all odds. In short, falling in love and getting out of it is a function of our own choice, our mind, and our brain, irrespective of the other person's nature, behaviour, character, personality, temperament, actions, deed, and conduct. The ball is in our court, boss, and we toss it into somebody else's court.'

Raj is thoughtful for a moment, and then he says, 'You do not sound like a nineteen-year-old.' His face lights up, and he says with a smile, 'Are you certain of your age? You should write this down in a diary.'

'Yes, Raj, I do write a diary. Raj, it is better to be with a person who loves you and not with the one you love. I would always want to be with the person who needs me the most rather than being with the one whom I need. I would like to wish you best of luck for your exams.'

'Shalinii, my mind is free of the confusion that lay there. There was a crowding of thoughts, and I could not deal with it. I feel vacant, like the empty sky after a heavy shower of rain when the black weighty clouds have shed off all that they have to. Thank you and bye.'

'Bye, Raj.'

I am reassured, and I walk towards my hostel and my room. The uncalled for burden on my head since morning has been offloaded, and I am basking in the glory of independence. It is a freedom from my thought process. I feel as if it is dawn, and I have just woken up from a sound, deep sleep, fresh and bright to start a new day. Though I have given a piece of advice to Raj, I am at peace with myself. The guilt which I felt when I looked at Raj every time has evaporated.

Life moves on. My medicine term of three months is about to get over. I learn the diagnostic and therapeutic procedures carried out on the human body. It is here that I learn to give intramuscular and intravenous injections. I begin to comprehend medical terminologies and their implications. I am a part of this world, and I feel I belong to the world of human physical and mental mysteries. The response of medicines on different people can be unpredictable, especially the side effects can be a wide spectrum, but they are mild, never life-threatening. The way people describe the complaints of their illnesses are disjointed and jumbled at times. The biggest test lies in deciphering local regional words and their meanings. Being a metro and the capital of a majestic state, Mumbai is the heartland of hundreds of different languages.

I have hardly met Pawan or Raj and Vishal who are busy with their exams. I spend most of my time studying in my room and watching television in the hostel. One fine Sunday morning, when I am languid, I receive a message in my room that somebody has come to meet me. I go down to the visitor's room to find an unknown person waiting there. I come out of the hostel searching for the right person. A senior girl tells me that my visitor is in the room itself. I go back to the room to find a slim man with a beard and white hair and moustache with strange curious eyes. He is about sixty years old and all bent over at the hip. That's my estimate; I am not an expert at it. I ask him, 'Who is it that you want to see?'

'I am here to meet a Miss Shalinii. Can you call her please?' I am uneasy and am not fine talking to this man. He looks very bizarre and unnatural to me. I decide not to disclose my identity on the spur of a moment.

'I am a friend of hers. She is not around. Is there some message that you would like me to pass on to her?' I question him.

'Where can I find her? I would like to meet her personally.' He gets up and is about to walk out when I interrupt him.

'Who was here do I tell her and for what?'

'I told you once, I am here to meet her. I will search for her in the canteen or library. Has she gone out?' He shouts loud enough to scare me once again. I nod my head in the negative and stand there like a statue not moving at all till he is out of my sight. I have kind of held my breath as he goes out. I slowly move out and up the stairs in the balcony of the second-floor corridor. I watch him walking on the pavement outside the hostel and am surprised. He walks briskly and straight, not at all like an old man. I am perspiring heavily. He gives me shivers. Who is he, and why does he want to meet me? The question troubles me a lot.

Simran comes to my room just then. I am relieved to see her. The tears I have so well tried to guard start flowing. Simran feels I am homesick, and I do not counter her. I talk to her in general for some time and dress up as soon as she goes out of the room. There has been an instance when I am about to spill the beans and tell Simran what I am going through. I change my mind as I start looking at each and every person with suspicion. I am in a mental state where I do not have faith on my own shadow. Something, a sixth sense, tells me I am in deep trouble. The man, whom I met a few minutes ago, haunts me. Am I becoming paranoid? I am asking myself. I go down to the reception with no particular agenda in mind. I am too scared to be in my room alone. Smriti is at her sister's place. As I saunter down the stairs in a trance, I see a figure at the huge wooden gate of my hostel. The face of the person looks familiar, but in my daze, I fail to recognize him. I keep staring at the smiling face with no expression on my own face. He walks towards me as soon as he sees me, and he is talking to me, but I fail to cognate the words falling on my ears. I am walking past him, and he shakes me up hard for me to finally respond. I come back to my senses when I see Pooja and two other girls staring at me with concern.

'Shalinii, have you taken some drugs?' Pooja asks.

Before I respond, the man holding me is quick to say, 'Pooja, she is under severe stress.'

'No, Pawan, I guess someone has drugged her,' Pooja adds.

I am wide awake as I hear Pawan's name. 'I am fine, Pooja, and I am not drugged, just going through hell at present. I shall be fine, do not worry.'

I am happy to see Pawan but confused at this accurate timing of his, being here when I most needed him. There is a warning bell in my brain which says, 'Beware. Pawan himself might be playing some games with you.' How can he do that? I know him well, and somewhere deep down, I admire him too. I stand there in that baffled state of mind, fear writ wide on my face. I want to know an answer, and I ask the foremost question going on in my mind to Pawan.

'How come you are at the hostel at this time?'

'I came to meet you.' He gives me a simple answer.

I am ready with my next question, and I shoot at him like a thunderbolt. 'Why?'

He looks around us. We are still standing at the hostel gate with an addition to the already existing audience surrounding us.

'Can we go out someplace and talk?' he requests coolly.

I am tempted to say no. I have to agree due to the condition I have put myself in. My thoughts are running haywire by now. Could Pawan be that old man in disguise and has now come to see the effects of his practical joke on me? For a split second, my anxiety is allayed. If the mysterious stalker is Pawan, I at least know it means no harm. A smile spreads across my face, fading away immediately as I feel unsafe and unsure. Would he really not harm me?

Why would he do that? I question myself, to gain what? What if he wants to harm me? I have walked into his plan successfully. I am alone with him.

I come out of my thoughts when he stands right across me, sweeping me into a gentle hug. He pulls my face close to his, kissing me on the forehead, whispers, 'I mean no harm, and I very well know what you are going through because I have met the man.'

My brain is again crowded with more doubts about Pawan and his intentions. He is aware of the man. Oh, so he sends this man and then comes to sympathize with me. How disgusting. I am looking at him with complete disbelief and distrust. We are now beyond the hearing range from the hostel, and I panic. I move away from him and am about to start running. Pawan senses what I am about to do. He holds my hand tightly and shouts loudly, 'For God's sake, don't behave childishly. I am not what you are thinking me to be. I was outside the canteen talking to Vishal when I saw this man enquiring about you, and his appearance caught my attention. I heard him say that you are not in the hostel, so I searched every corner of the college for you and then came here to find out where you were. The state you are in gave me the clue that you have somehow met that man. I did not want to discuss this at the hostel, and I brought you here. I did not speak to him as I did not want him to see me. Please calm down, and do not lose your self-control. We will find out who he is and what he has to do with you. I have asked Kelvin to follow him while I am here.'

'Pawan, I have not known this man. I do not know why he wants to meet me, and I am afraid of him. Who could he be?'

'We will go back to college and wait for Kelvin in the library. Have you taken your breakfast?'

'Forget breakfast, I have not even had my bath. I was just lazing around in my room trying to study the effects of the anticholinergic drugs when this man came. I guessed my maternal uncle was here to see me and rushed to the visitor's room. I did not like him and did not reveal my identity. I lied to him that I was Shalinii's friend and I could pass on a message from him to her. He insisted on meeting me personally and reprimanded me to shut up. Tell me, Pawan, did he not look odd?'

'Yes, he did, and that is why I am concerned. This is Mumbai dear, and anything can happen here. We will eat first and then go to the library where you can continue reading anticholinergics, and I shall go through the latest surgical magazines.'

'Are you interested in surgery?' I ask him with astonishment.

'Yes, I always have been a strong surgical candidate. I love to operate upon a patient. I mean, there is such a relief the patient gets after an emergency much-needed surgery. It is a magical transformation in the life of that patient.'

'That happens with the medical line of treatment also. You can see patients getting well even with medicines.'

'Medical management has its limitations.'

'You think surgery does not have any limitations. I always felt you would be interested in paediatrics.'

'Surgery has its own limitations. But our work starts after your medicines fail to cure a person. What made you think I was interested in paediatrics?'

'I sensed you love children.'

'How did you sense that?'

'Then why do you go to an orphanage once in a while?'

'Who told you that?' He was bowled over by my unexpected attack.

'I saw you walk out of Balgram one day when I had gone in the neighbouring cake shop on Smriti's birthday last year. I asked the watchman out of curiosity, and he told me you visit there once in a while.'

He dropped his guard and whispered, 'You are the first one to have found this out. It is not something to be kept as a secret. But you know my reputation in college, do you not? I am supposed to be a rough-and-tough guy. I do not want to expose this side of me. Do you mind if I smoke? I need a cigarette urgently, too many things to deal with at one go.'

'Why do you smoke, and is there some reason you visit Balgram?'

'Shalinii, are you aware that you are a difficult person to be with since you ask too many questions?'

'I am aware, but I am waiting for your answers right now.'

We are by now comfortably sitting in the canteen, enjoying our food. I am out of the tensions due to the happenings of the early morning.

'My mother expired when I was ten years old. She had cancer of the kidney with no major symptoms. The diagnosis was done in the later stages, and she could not be saved. My father loved her a lot. He pushed himself into business full-time after that, and I was left all alone. My father died when I was in second MB in a car accident. I am an orphan myself, and I identify with those kids out there. They are like a family to me, and I take pleasure in being with them. That is exactly the time when I broke up with Shipra and took to smoking. It is a difficult addiction to give up.'

'With a history of cancer in the family, don't you think smoking would predispose you to lung cancer? I am sorry about your parents. Do you have any siblings?' I am tempted to ask him about his former girlfriend but leave it to be conferred upon some other time. He is in a good disposition, and I do not want to spoil our current equation.

'Shalinii', he takes a deep exasperated breath before he starts speaking, 'I have no real brother or sister, a lot of caring cousins and uncles and aunts. I want to give up this habit, but it has become a part of my survival.'

We enter the library after eating. I am sitting in a chair with my book, and he goes to the journals section to go through the dull literature. The library closes at 4 p.m. as it is a Sunday, and as we are walking out of it, Kelvin meets us.

'I followed him up to Dharavi, and then he disappeared in one of the by-lanes into a shanty,' Kelvin tells us.

'Dharavi is the biggest slum of Asia, and he has gone there, which means nuisance for us. Shalinii, you will have to be careful until we get what he was here to meet you for. I am going to see the place in Dharavi and make some enquiries about our mystery man in the neighbourhood. You go back to the hostel. Don't venture out alone anywhere and even while coming to college, come with your group as always. In case of any emergency, just reach the boys' hostel and ask for help. All the boys in there are good and would not deter from helping you.'

'Shouldn't we be reporting to the police and taking their help?' Kelvin says to us.

'What will we tell the police, and what if they don't take us seriously? We will make that man alert, and he might prove to be more treacherous. We have to first find out why he was here and what all this is for. We will leave you at your hostel gate.'

As I am entering my room, Pooja follows close on my heels. She latches the door from inside and demands, 'Shalinii, what is going on? I have been waiting for you since some time. Where were you? I am not so sure of Pawan. There are stories making the rounds that he used to hit his former girlfriend black and blue and so she broke with him. He could be into drugs. He is popular but infamous in college. Are you in love with him? He is too proud to visit our hostel unless there is a strong reason for him to do so.'

'I am not in love. He was here to meet me and warn me about something.' I am tempted to tell the happenings of that day to Pooja. I maintain my silence though. How much ever you swear a person to secrecy, stories spread like wildfire in this hostel. Girls cannot keep things to themselves.

'A thief comes to warn people to lock their houses,' she says with sarcasm. I do not like the way she talks about Pawan. It is her outlook, and I do not care. She moves out of my room, realizing I would not disclose anything. I close the door behind her. My thoughts come back to me.

I have read in most crime books that the culprit is the person closest to the victim or the one who is the least suspected person. My mind reflects the happenings of the entire day and many more days prior to this day to get answers to a lot of questions. I am again at a loss and am suspicious of everybody around me. Pawan is a sadist; he could do anything. Could it be Raj's doing? Some other boys from my class who were on the verge of proposing me, or some friend from the hostel whom I may have hurt unknowingly? I stretch and strain my brain to find a loophole, and I find many. I fall asleep with my thoughts.

The heavy knock on my door wakes me up, and as I open the door, the girl announces 'Visitor for you' and disappears down the corridor before I thank her or recognize her. I look out of my window, and it is dark outside and the word *visitor* sends me into a cold sweat with shivers. I call a junior next to my room and send her to the visitor's room to inquire who it is. She comes back and tells me it is Pawan. I reluctantly go down to meet him. I enter the room to find four people seated there.

Pawan speaks up no sooner than I am in the room. 'Shalinii, I and Kelvin visited the place. It is in the heart of Dharavi. We went through dirty discoloured, grey, dark lanes and by-lanes to reach this really shabby shanty which was locked. Upon enquiring into the neighbourhood, we got a range of answers. An old man with a limp stays there, and he keeps to himself most of the time. The description fits the person you and I met today. People have seen a nurse walk in and out of the place in the nurse's uniform. This is the only link you could have. She could be the oldie's daughter. One more person visits the place. He could be the old man's son. He has a supposedly criminal background. He is a pickpocket and commits small crimes like stealing household items. I do not find any connection between you and this threesome though. Have you ever visited Dharavi or known anyone from there?'

'Pawan, I do not know where Dharavi is, and I do not know anybody in this city other than people from our college. Why did you bring these two in their exam term?' I ask, looking at Raj and Vishal who have been the mute spectators of our talk.

'Shalinii, I know you cannot trust anyone at this moment. I did not want this to be between you and me alone. I would advise you to inform this to at least two girls from your hostel whom you trust.'

'Why do we not take the help of the police or inform her parents about it? This could be related to her family, you never know.' Kelvin is annoyed at having got involved into this. He wants to put the responsibility off his shoulders.

'No, her parents will unnecessarily be troubled,' Raj speaks for the first time.

'I spoke to my parents yesterday. There was nothing unusual. If some specific incident would have occurred with them there, I would have been the first person to be informed. I do not think this man has anything to do with them.' At this time, I take an important decision, and I continue to talk. 'I trust you completely, Pawan. I require no alibis. Raj and Vishal, we will update you from time to time, and only Pawan and I will continue to investigate this matter. I am not informing any more people. You all can go back. I shall be very careful, and let's wait and watch without making any fuss about it. Bye, guys, and thanks for your help and concern. I really appreciate that, and it means a lot to me. Bye.' I go up the staircase without waiting for them to move out of the hostel. Once in my room, I am doing my homework of going through my memory for a possible clue linking the facts with some past incidence of my life.

It is a terrible mental exercise looking for suspects when there are none or maybe everyone in my life. I scan distant relatives, acquaintances, associates of my father or my uncles, etc. But I am blank. I see no face of crime around me in all these years of my being. It strikes me that my father had been a professor and a very strict one too. He would be on squads during exams to inspect examination centres and a few students had been debarred from giving exams because of him. Could this be some disgruntled student of his? It is a farfetched possibility which could not be denied.

I am going through the events of the evening, and something does not feel right to me. Pawan seems overly concerned. I cannot make out whether it is a mask or if he is genuinely worried. Raj seems too detached; could be as a result of his exam, but his coolness is agonizing me. Vishal has been without any reaction. These are a few of my best friends. Either they do not comprehend what is happening and what to do or maybe they are the culprits. I have seen Raj and Pawan get even with each other once. Any of them could trouble me to hurt the other. Should I talk to Vidya and Simran about this whole affair? They are there in the hostel today. They stayed because we have a forensic and pharmacology viva tomorrow that I had completely forgotten about. I decide to revise for the viva. I refrain from talking to them until after the exams.

The viva the next day are a catastrophe. As it is, I have revulsion to viva. Before I have a chance to talk to my friends about the mystery man, another misfortune strikes us. Mandar and Sushant, while returning back from their relatives' place on a bike, meet with an accident. It is not a major one. Mandar has a head injury which is not deep. He has to undergo a CAT scan to rule out internal injury. He has contused lacerated wounds (CLW) at three places, including one on the scalp which requires surgical suturing. Sushant has a fracture of his left arm. They are admitted in the orthopaedic ward for observation. All of us rush there after college, take turns to be with them, and provide them with food and water. It is fine to treat patients, but being a patient is distasteful. After the first aid and plaster, they want to seek the cosiness of their room. Being students of the college with no guardians is a big responsibility on the treating doctors. They are not ready for any compromise in the management of these VIP patients. Reluctantly, the two have to oblige when the HOD insists that they stay in the hospital. We make it into a picnic of sorts for them, and they enjoy their accident and their stay in the biggest general hospital of India.

The next two to three days are without any incidence. I get into my routine stuff and start to concentrate on my studies. I spend most of the time in the library along with Vidya and Simran. I have still not been able to make myself pour my heart out to my friends. The reason behind not informing them about the incident is they, being girls, are emotional and would get worked up. We have our first-term exams approaching in no time.

CHAPTER TWELVE

I have been reading my diary the whole day, and it is close to midnight. The enthusiasm to continue reading is very high. I am tired beyond limits in this journey down memory lane. I have watched a movie of my own life on this day. It has been too much of a mental exercise reliving all those moments again as though they are just happening now, in front of my eyes.

The whole week after the storm is dedicated to the revival of the whole town. The municipal head of the town of Dhadgaon is a woman for the first time in the history of this town. She is a schoolteacher and a friend of mine. Seema is her name, and she is in her current position on my recommendation. People of the town wanted me to take this position. It would not have been possible for me to take any further responsibilities other than my professional commitments. I suggested her name and promised to back her up and help her in every possible way when the need arose. I have to stand by my word now, and we indeed do a fantastic job in getting things back to normal in the presence of all odds. Most men in the political fraternity have been supportive of our work on the face. Somewhere deep within themselves, they are not ready to accept female supremacy and leadership.

Our culture, our epics, our heritage are male dominant. A society in which the females do not deny themselves to be the weaker segment of the universe, where a mother teaches her daughter that her male counterpart is her god and she has to agree to his supremacy by default. What can be done? This is rural India, though the urban India is no different. When females have been rebellious, the picture is ruinous. It shakes the basic foundation of human existence. What is then at the core of the coexistence of the two genders on earth? The answer to this question is very simple, not easy to follow, and each of us knows the answer. Unconditional love and respect for each other at all times is the key to the biggest riddle of any relationship.

We too have our share of dominance on us which we overcome intelligently. Nobody here opposes us, but we are challenged to fail in our task every minute. It is not that we do not fall prey to their backbiting. We fall and we rise and we fall and rise again, we keep falling and then rising, thus we rise and rise and develop into the ones who are focused on what we have to do versus being unsure of ourselves. The town is back to normal with its vigour and vitality in no time. I am at the heart of all the happenings and have achieved profound happiness.

It is the way we look at things. I could have been crying sad, lonely, dejected being a divorcee and for having lost the love of my life. I might have ruined my life doing nothing significant and here I am at the source of the existence of so many and many more lives. Pawan is with me as a part of my life, for my sake, though in reality, he is not around me. He exists in my thoughts, gestures, and strength and in my power to take on the world. Before I realize it, it is Sunday, and I await the arrival of Vishal.

There has been no communication between me and Vishal in the past one week. I am sure Vishal would come today, and I do not keep any engagements for the day. I designate work to people around me, being available on the phone in case of an emergency. The weather is clear since the past four days. There is no chance that Vishal would miss this appointment whatever the weather conditions may be. How he found me out in this silent corner of the world after so many years is a mystery to me. I get a strange feeling in my stomach since morning. I am excited and nervous at the same time. How will I face Vishal? I wonder what it would be like if I come face to face with either Pawan or Raj. How would I confront those two? I am keeping my nerves under check. I wake up early and am ready before 10 a.m.

The condition in which I am at present reminds me of the bygone days. I have seen cousins elder to me in this state when eligible bachelors along with families would be invited, and they came home to see, meet, and visit them for the first time. There is the excitement of meeting a soulmate and the tension of meeting a stranger and his family for the first time. The anxiety is also for the reason that all should go well during the visit with both the parties being cordial to each other. Vishal is no stranger for me; meeting him after years when the world has moved a full circle as a result of the advanced technologies is troubling me. I feel like a frog in the pond about to meet a frog from the sea. I am surprised at my own activities. It is as though a representative of Pawan is coming to meet me.

I have especially invited Parvati to cook lunch. I sit in my bedroom doing nothing in particular other than looking at myself in the mirror. Do I look old? Have I gained too much weight? Will Vishal recognize me? What would be his first reaction on meeting me? I am preparing myself to meet the person who has been my best friend and also that of my ex- husband. I am going through the longest hour of my life, eager to hear some news about Pawan. The alarm for 11 a.m. today that I had set before, starts ringing, and it awakens me from my thoughts. The clock moves very slowly with me counting every second of the time thereafter. It is eleven fifteen and then thirty and then quarter to twelve with no signs of either Vishal or his phone. It is 1 p.m., and I am still waiting. I start losing hope.

Hope is something that all of us are living on. The hope of a better tomorrow, the hope of someday reaching our destination, the hope of fulfilling our dreams; hope drives us through our days and nights. Ask an infertile couple hoping for a child, a child about his hopes to grow up fast. A blind man hopes to see the world with his own eyes. A young man hopes to get married to his beloved. A person just broken from a relationship hopes to find a better life partner. The poor hope for money and the rich for peace of mind. The uneducated keep hoping to learn new things, and the educated go on hoping for a job. A lovesick girl longing for her lover, the hopes of soldiers on the border to go on a vacation to meet their family, endless number of people hoping for infinite things in their lives. It is a never-concluding tale of hopes. Hoping for something is the reason for many people to be alive. Hope is fine. But hope blinding the veracity is troublesome. Hoping to not accept the known reality is lunacy. It is like living a fallacious life. Where does this hope lead to? Debacle and we name it misfortune. There is no hope in death. Hoping beyond that is not viable, and we still hope to achieve that, to live on forever. We pour our hearts out claiming to be unlucky. Hope without consistent efforts will take us nowhere.

At that realization, I think of calling up Vishal on his cell phone. The doorbell of my house rings just then, I get cold feet. I keep sitting, expecting Parvati to open the door. She comes in the bedroom and announces, 'Two men to see you, madam.'

'Ask them to sit in the front room and offer them water while I come there,' I reply with my mind stuck at the *two* that Parvati says. Who has come with Vishal? Could it be Pawan? How could he fly across continents at such a short notice? I brush the thought aside. Vishal must have brought along a friend instead of travelling alone.

I enter the room where the two of them have been sitting, I cry out loud astonished, 'I never expected to see you here, Raj.'

'Raj does not forget his friends as easily as they do. I am here today because my wife sent me.'

'Oh! How are you, Vishal?' We had sort of ignored his presence completely as usual. 'How's Vidya, Raj?'

'I am fine, Shalinii, and Vidya has become very plump. She is a mother of two lovely sons who resemble Raj completely,' Vishal answers for himself as well as Raj. We are all very thrilled, and we start to talk all at the same time. Most of them are enquiries made about each other's lives.

'How's Pawan, Vishal?' I ask, and there is silence in the room all of a sudden.

'We have not heard much about him, Shalinii. We have got his address and the phone number of the place where he works. When we called him up last week, he was on a fortnightly vacation starting from that day. We do not know his current location and have to await his return to the hospital,' Raj replies instead of Vishal.

There is stillness in the room. Each of us has a thousand questions to ask the others. We stare at one another, not knowing where to begin and what to talk about. We are lost in thought, and we are trying to gather the threads of our lives from where we once left them. We collectively had been so much a part of the HP family and it's culture, but at this moment we are struggling to establish a connection between us. I nonchalantly ask them, 'When is the get together?'

'It is on 30 December.'

'It is a memorable date. Who decided it? Vidya, I guess.'

'No, it was not Vidya, I decided the date,' Raj says.

'It is Mandy's birthday. So we will be celebrating his birthday.' I say this, remembering Mandar, who had become Mandy for us.

'You do remember the date, Shalinii. I thought you must have forgotten.'

'Raj, I have not forgotten anything. How could I? He was my rakhi brother. After our third MBBS exam, just when we were to go on a vacation, Vidya, Mandy and I met for the last time. He told us he was leaving for Solapur, his home town, in the evening and that he would never ever come back to Mumbai. I insisted, you have to come to take your results, and he said he would not. Vidya had not committed to him for a relationship, and he was uneasy. He said he would go off to USA. When I asked him what he would do about his internship, he said he would take an externship to Solapur medical college. I sent him a greeting card for his birthday from home via post. You called me to give the sad news of his accidental death on 14th of January, and can you imagine the irony when I received a letter written by him in reply to my greetings on 15th of January? I thought it was a bad joke that you had played on me until I went to Solapur and met his aggrieved family.'

'Shalinii, you have indeed matured. You could not talk about Mandy without tears in your eyes and look at you now.'

'What do I have in my hands today other than remembering people as happy memories? My tears have been replaced by a plastered smile on my face. Who all do I cry for Mandy, Pawan, Raj, Vishal, Vidya, Simran, Pooja, Smriti, and so many others? It is a never-ending list of people. I miss all of you.'

'Why did you stop communicating?'

'I was in communication with Simran and Poonam till I left USA. After coming back to India, I was not sure where I would settle. When I reached here, I created a new world for myself, and I felt I would be happy not being in communication with all those who knew Pawan. It is as if I wanted to obliterate my past and Pawan.'

'Just a minute, let's rewind a bit. Shalinii, as far as I remember, I have talked to the two of you the day you left for Chandigarh. What happened after that? Pawan told me he would send me the address of your residence as soon as he joined Chandigarh medical college, and I have been waiting for it till date.' Vishal's question once again leaves me speechless. So many years have passed in between, and I do not know what to say.

'Wait, I was not there the day you all left, practically speaking I have not spoken to you since you got married.

Pawan had his MS exam, and I did not want to disturb him, so I did not contact you. I was busy with my residency at St. Peter's Hospital.'

'Yes, Raj, that is true. You finished your internship by the time I joined mine after passing my third year exam and you went for your postgraduation to St Peter's and Vishal went to Swami Vivekananda Medical College. Pawan was doing general surgery at H.P. itself. We each moved towards our destined future.'

'Pawan has been a lucky guy. He got to do postgraduation in the subject he wanted that too at HP. I was interested in paediatrics but had to be content with general medicine. Vishal wanted to do anaesthesia and has ended up with pathology. You had been a gynaecology and obstetrics candidate since first year, and you did paediatrics.'

'Raj, it is how you take it. I am happy having been a paediatrician. We have to be content and satisfied with what we are doing. We got our basic degrees then, how to paint and create our life's canvas later on is up to us. Vidya also got her PG in general medicine at your hospital, and you came close to each other and are married today. What more do you expect in life?'

Parvati walks in. This is a signal for me that food is ready, and it is time to have lunch. I go in the kitchen to find the table set for food. I come out into the sitting room and declare to the two of them, 'Lunch is ready to be served, we better have food first.'

'Forget the food, answer our questions first, we have the whole of the rest of our lives to eat.'

'Come on, let's eat, I am already hypoglycaemic, my blood sugar has gone down, and I need to eat before I get a migraine. Then I shall begin from the beginning. Please freshen up and come to the dining table.' Saying this, I stroll into the kitchen, leaving them with no other option than to follow my instructions.

'Aha! It is baingan ka bharta, Pawan's favourite dish,' exclaims Raj.

'There is also this special kheer that he so relishes. Tell me, Shalinii, did you for once feel I would bring him along?' This is Vishal's question.

'Yes, to be honest, and when I was told there were two visitors, I felt sure.'

'Sorry to have disappointed you, I asked for his family or residential phone number. They said he is a private person and would not like them to divulge any information about him. I have been helpless. I was forced to bring in Raj as I did not have the nerve to stand alone in front of you.'

'Why? It's fine with me. I have waited for him since ages. I feel someday I shall meet him, at least before I die. Maybe few years down the line when we grow old and he visits India, we will be able to see each other. He must have fathered a child by now, could be two children, I do not know. I am longing to see his children once. Genes express themselves perfectly well, and it would be fun to watch Pawan's Xerox copies.' The ease with which I talk shocks the two men present in the room with me.

'Shalinii, you have not answered my question, why did you isolate yourself and go into self-exile?'

'Raj, I am coming to that. When Pawan and I separated, I came back to India.'

'Shalinii, you have already told us that.'

'Raj, will you be patient and let her talk. It is not painless for her to tell us about Pawan.'

'Actually, I do not know where to begin. I will first answer your question. Raj, tell me, if you or any of my close friends would have known that Pawan and I have separated, what would you have done? Would you not have tried to bring us together?'

'Oh! Shalinii, do you have to ask that? The reply is an obvious yes.'

'Relationship is between two individuals. How to maintain it is their prerogative. Well-wishers can advise, request, influence, and try to amend the bond. The outlook of the two towards that association and their rapport with each other determines the existence of that connection. Any other person is a third person who cannot make a marked difference in the day-to-day, moment-to-moment endurance of the affiliation between them. This is true for any relationship.'

I pause and take a deep breath. Parvati is serving us and acts as a physical distraction for me intermittently. She is nowhere near to being a part of our conversation as she does not understand English. I have kept Pawan's photographs safely locked in the cupboard. She does not know I was married once. I am uncomfortable lest my treasured secret be disclosed in my present surroundings. I continue further giving up that thought.

'Would you not have been hurt? You would have even pitied me. By *you*, I mean any of my acquaintances. I did not want to go into a state of self-pity. If ten people would have shown me sympathy, I would have lost my self-confidence. Today I can talk about my break-up with Pawan like a passer-by or observer. At that time, I was completely devastated. It was the stage of my life when I could not imagine my life without him. It was a fresh trauma for me, and any psychological insult, though not meant to be, would have been detrimental to my ego and pride. I preferred going into a shell, into seclusion to heal myself and to learn to smile again. You would have helped me. I had to learn to live, to love myself first. I blamed myself for the failure of our relationship. It was meant to be that way and was not under my control. I felt responsible for whatever wrong happened between me and Pawan. It was all about me, and I was not ready to look beyond myself. Some external force bringing me out of that phase would have been temporary. I had to become strong myself, from within, to come out of that phase and emerge as a powerful being.'

We finish our lunch. I take a deep sigh of relief to get out of the kitchen away from Parvati and her hearing range. I am not willing to share my past with a person who was not a part of it. As we settle down in the hall, Vishal comes up with the next question. As he opens his mouth to talk, I laugh nervously and say, 'The feeling that I am getting is that of being interviewed by the press. Since you are Pawan's friends, it is as if he is the victim of circumstances and I am trying to prove my innocence.'

'Shalinii, you are being paranoid. We are your friends too. We are talking to you keeping the interests of both of you in front of us. Do not go into a negative mindset. We want to get to the root of the discord between the two of you,' Raj says it with real feelings for us.

'Exactly and that is what I want to know, Shalinii, what went wrong between you and Pawan?' Vishal asks what I had predicted to be the purpose of their visit.

'Well, Pawan loved me a lot whilst in India. When we set our foot in the USA, all was well initially. Slowly but surely over passing days, he distanced himself from me. I failed to understand the reason of his behaviour, and I would coax him to spend time with me. He became very moody. It took my life out of me to see him suffer. He never told me what he was going through and why. We were drifting apart, at least he was. He became aloof and started coming home late at night. I would be waiting for him for dinner, and he would have already finished it before coming home. I would be up almost the whole night out of worry and tension. I had insomnia, I would go to sleep in the early morning and by the time I woke up, he would have left for work. We hardly interacted with each other for days together. On weekends too he would not be in the house. I thought he had a major depression, not being able to cope up with the work pressures in the USA. I had a reason to think that way. He would be crying at times all by himself.'

My voice deepens, and I seem to be on the verge of crying. I am going through the ordeal of those days again. I recollect everything but pull myself from there as if waking from a bad dream. I gather myself and continue to talk, more to myself than to Raj and Vishal.

'He became short tempered, started shouting at me, abusing me verbally without any reason or provocation. All this while, I did my best to understand him and be with him. Then one day, he hit me in a fit of rage. I lost my patience and asked him what was all this. He said he was in love with a beautiful and lovely American lady, a nephrologist, working with him, a part of his research team. He wanted to divorce me and marry her. I got the answers to my question. I booked a flight back to India, packed my bags, signed the divorce papers without reading them, and left USA for better.' My voice is heavy again, and my respiration deep and irregular. I make an attempt to smile and fail miserably in it.

'Did you not ask him what you are to do after leaving him?' Raj shouts angrily, loud enough to bring me into the present immediately.

'Do you think that would have made any difference Raj? He did not love me anymore. That was sufficient for me to withdraw from his life. He had taken his decision, and I had to take mine. Can you force someone to love you?'

'Shalinii, you should not have walked off so easily from his life. How do you know he is in safe hands? Did you meet the lady? How is it possible that one can stop loving? Love is eternal, non-ending. It is a function of additions, not subtraction. You can love more and more people but cannot delete the ones who are already there in your life. A man cannot stop loving his father with the birth of his daughter. He has to expand to accommodate both of them.'

'I did not find it necessary to meet her. He was spending a lot of time with her. I could not have begged him to leave her. I was like a hindrance in his path. He would have hated me more. The most sensible thing for me to do then was to leave him. Do you want to say that he should have stayed with me and had an affair with her?'

'No, that is not what I meant, Shalinii. She could have been his friend, and he could have continued being a responsible husband. He cannot compromise one relationship to justify the other. You were his first priority no matter what.'

Vishal has been listening silently all this while. He seems to be deep in some thought. He says, 'Shalinii, did you want to go to the US? What were you doing there? I mean professionally.'

'You know we left Mumbai when my internship was over and Pawan had finished his MS general surgery. I was a medical graduate and he a postgraduate. Pawan wanted to do his MCh Urology, which is a super specialty course, and he got admission in Chandigarh medical college, which has the best urology centre in India. He wanted us to get married before he left, and so we got married towards the end of my internship. He took me along with him to Chandigarh where after passing the common entrance test of that college I took up paediatrics. We stayed together and worked in the same premises. All was well. When I passed my MD paediatrics exam, he had passed his MCh. He had applied for a fellowship in the UK. But his boss at Chandigarh recommended him to one of his counterpart and friend in the USA. Pawan was selected to work there, and we left India. We had not planned it in advance. Pawan did want to go to the USA. It would be so soon is what none of us had foreseen. I had to take the US MLE, which is their entrance exam, and do a postgraduate course there. I had applied for the upcoming exam and was preparing for it.'

'You are not telling me if you were happy there.'

'I was with the person I loved the most, I was happy there. At least one of us was following his dreams.'

'Shalinii, as far as I know Pawan, he had great value for every person in his life. He loved you much before he confessed to you and proposed you. This is not expected of him. It is not that I do not believe you, but there is a missing link. Why did you not talk to him? What do you mean by one of us? This clearly shows you were not happy.'

'I tried talking to him. But he would not be home, Vishal. I did not care for my damn happiness even once. I was all the time with him, supporting him like a solid rock through thick and thin. I never complained.'

'You should have gone over to his workplace. Your pride was hurt to such an extent with the knowledge of there being someone else in his life that you turned your back on him never to return again. Don't you think you should have been in touch with him? You wanted to prove it to yourself to satisfy your ego that if he does not require you in his life, you also do not need him. You crying here thinking of him as if he were dead is imprudent.'

'Vishal, how can you justify Pawan's conduct? You cannot censure her for what she did. How are you doing at present, Shalinii?' Raj's apprehension is discernible by the way he switches the topic.

'I have made myself useful to those who need me, and I keep myself engaged from dawn to dusk. I have no time to ponder over my past. I am looking forward to a very bright future of this town.'

It is teatime, Parvati has left, and I go to the kitchen to prepare tea. I hear an argument between Raj and Vishal. I ignore it. The volume of their words goes on increasing, as I come out with the tea cups in hand.

'The two of you shouldn't be fighting over me and Pawan. We were each justified and correct in what we did. Your interception is not going to change our lives. You live your lives happily. You can be in touch with me as well as Pawan. I have no bad feelings for him. I wouldn't mind meeting him as an old friend someday. Arrange the get together. I am looking forward to seeing all our friends. I would like to celebrate Mandy's birthday and give him my good wishes wherever he is.'

We sip our tea quietly. I take Raj and Vishal for a tour of the town. I take on the role of a tourist guide, showing them proudly the new creations in Dhadgaon. I feel like a child who has scored well in the exams showing his report card to his parents.

Raj and Vishal prepare to leave. I want them to stay over. I want to talk to them. I cannot bring myself to tell them to be with me for some more time. The climatic conditions are not very favourable. I do not want them to be stuck here away from their families. With a heavy heart I give them permission to leave, and they drive back, promising to be here with their families in the next vacation. I go back into the empty house and the emptiness of my life. Discussing my friends' lives and their families is the incentive for me to live until their next visit.

I go into a lot of negativism that evening. Why did I not make attempts to salvage my marriage? Was I really unsighted with self-pride? Should I communicate with Pawan? Is it not too late? There is no point in telling Pawan now how much I love and miss him. He has moved on in life. I should have acted then. The time has now passed away. We cannot go back in time. It is necessary to take action at the right time, and time does not wait for anybody. The moment I reached a conclusion to come back to India, I lost my battle with time. Retrospectively looking at it, it was as if I was waiting for that decision of mine. I had never wanted to go to the US. I have been too patriotic since childhood to leave the country I was born in. There had been a complete shift in my persona since I married Pawan. I dumped all my aspirations and wishes down the drain. I went on to follow Pawan's dreams. I thought that was the right thing for me to do, but somewhere, I was not happy. I tried to deter Pawan from going to a foreign land. Pawan had been interested in research work and scientific experimentation. According to him, it would not be feasible for him to do it with the limited resources in India. We are ten years behind the west in research and development of newer techniques in any field he would say. The rest of my day passes in self-introspection with no concrete outcome. I am about to put the lights of my bedroom off for the night. There is a knock on my door. I open the door to find an unknown man standing in the doorway and a shiny red Mercedes car standing in the driveway.

'Who are you, and why are you here?' I ask him as politely as I can.

'Madam, Mr Ramdas sent me to fetch you to his bungalow. I am his driver cum secretary.'

'Who is this Mr Ramdas? Do I know him?'

'Everybody knows him. He is the standing MLA of this place.'

'Oh! Oh yes, I do know him,' I say as I mentally visualize the man I have met occasionally and shared the dais with.

'Is some small child not well in his house? You should bring the child to the hospital rather than me coming to his house. You see, I would not have much to do at home. Can you bring the child to Mandar hospital? I will reach there if he wants me to examine the child,' I say as a routine, having faced this kind of a situation many times previously. There would be a doctor on call, but they insist on me seeing the patient, and most of the time, I do it willingly.

'No Madam, nobody is ill.' He continues ahead, looking at the bewilderment on my face, 'He wants to talk to you about something very important and urgent.'

'What can be so urgent? Is somebody's life in danger? If no, then please ask him to see me at Mandar hospital at 11 a.m. tomorrow.'

I shut the door without waiting for an answer. I proceed to my bedroom as I hear the starting of the car engine. My thought process goes into action. What is the work that this man, known well in the area to be a shrewd politician, have with me? Does it have to do with the hospital that is being planned? Why did he send a person home at this hour? Why should I go to his house? Did I do the right thing by not going, or should I have gone? We act in a particular fashion, think about the whys, ifs, and buts later on. I will get to know the next day about this visit; till then I have to be patient. It does not serve to get worked up. If only I knew what is it, that is of significance to him, I could have geared up and equipped myself in advance to tackle him. He is a man who would not waste his resources on somebody without a tangible advantage to him. Since he sent his car, it has to be a matter of great interest to him. I go scanning through my memory to find a person who is on good terms with me and him. I am asleep before I get the reply.

The next morning, at eleven as I am busy with my OPD, Sister Ruby comes and tells me, 'Mr Ramdas to see you, madam.'

'Send him in after I finish with this patient.'

In another five minutes, the man is ushered into my room. He demonstrates power in his being. Dressed typically like most from his clan, he is in striking white clothes. A kurta and a pajama well ironed with not many creases yet which means I am his first stop this morning before proceeding to his durbar as people call it. The gold that he wears on his person must weigh in kilograms. He enters with an air of arrogance. His bodyguard follows, but he orders him to wait outside the room. I cannot tolerate this superciliousness. His endeavour in life is to be in the limelight at all times; I shun away from public eye. He is seated in front of me in no time and looks at me straight in the eye.

'I am not going to beat around the bush. Coming straight to the purpose of my visit, have you met Hemant?'

I do not recollect who he is. I infer it to be his son as I bring to mind the posters on the street on my way to the hospital. 'I have not met him or talked to him in person. I have seen his photographs.'

'That is as much as is necessary to set off at present. You have developed an eternal bond with this town. People hold you at a high esteem and admire you as god. My son would be standing for the elections due this year. I want you to help us out.'

'You are doing good work for the people. I would not mind campaigning for you and your party.'

'That is not what I want you to do. You have the prosperity of this town in mind. We too are working to achieve the same. Our destination is the same, we can do the journey together.'

'What do you mean?' I fail to decipher the deeper context behind his comment.

'Ideally, I would have talked to an elder person from your family. You are grown up and independent, so I thought of talking to you directly. Please marry my son.'

'What, what are you talking about, Mr Ramdas?' I see my temper rising up. I slowly count one to ten and take a deep breath to cool myself before resuming my words again. I talk as casually as possible. 'Tell me, Mr Ramdas, how old is your son?'

'He could be your age.'

'Mr Ramdas, your son is less than thirty-five years old, and I am forty plus. He would not want to get married to a woman older than his age. I had speculated he was already married.'

'He was married once, his wife died in an accident few years ago. You do not look old at all, and he is not of the mentality to deny you in marriage for being a few years older than him. I have talked to him prior to coming here.'

'Oh! I am sorry I was not aware about his wife's tragedy. I am already married. My husband is in the USA. He is into research and has not found time to come here. He is due to come any time now.' I speak whatever comes to my mind without thinking. I had decided not to get married again the day I signed the divorce papers.

'Are you sure you are married? Your age is no problem. Hemant would be glad to see you as his mother as well.'

I am astounded to such a degree that I do not trust my own ears. What this respectable man from the society is putting forward to me is difficult for me to digest. I am in command of my irritability once again with due efforts.

'You are proposing to a married woman half your age. Are you out of your psyche to do that?' I am not only talking loudly but am trembling and shaking. My blood pressure must have risen by a few millimeters at that moment.

'Bye, Mr Ramdas. If there is anything else I can do for you, you are most welcome. I love my husband very much and am happily married.' I get up from my seat and walk Mr Ramdas to the door.

Ruby walks past him into the room as he leaves. 'Beware of this kind of men, madam. They are sweet tongued, white outside, and black inside. They have their own welfare in their blood. These sharks are to be seen everywhere these days.'

'It is okay with me. I have learnt to deal with them over days. Do not fret, Ruby. I have developed an expertise in the field of human mannerism and their tendency of narrow-mindedness. I should be doing a PhD on human psychology and its pitfalls.' Both of us laugh at the joke and proceed on to the next waiting child patient.

I love children for their innocence and purity of thoughts. They are like God; everything is equal in their eyes. No dissimilarity within humans and between animals, plants, or birds. For them the smallest of things is of great value. They have a restricted view to life but completeness in each of their relationships, happy in their ignorance, free from precincts, ready to expand beyond the horizons. I wanted to take up being a doctor of the women. If I have an access to the woman and her attention, the whole family could be influenced, I thought. In my experience, this concept of mine has proved to be wrong. Our ideas and opinions vary constantly with the evidence presenting itself to us. Children have better control over a household. They are intelligent to mould the elders with an innovative, futuristic, revolutionary vision. We underestimate their might and restrict their autonomy, in effect cutting off their wings before they have learnt to fly fully. We dump our understandings of the world on them without letting them explore, observe, and scrutinize their environs through their own angle. Our race thus exhibits and attests itself to be self-extinct. Why do we require nuclear weapons? We want them to wrestle our own kin. We then hunt for happiness and peace of mind akin to gazing at the sun with a torch in the noon.

My life in this small town has a set tone. I do not allow it to become monotonous though. I am at the source of creating happiness. The power of which makes me insatiable for creativity and longevity further than my age and ability. People think I take a potion for youthfulness. I do take a potion, a potion of my nothingness and flexibility, of freedom and coexistence, of giving up and letting go, of contribution through competition, and of smile- and laughter-filled days. This town has had a makeover to become a place of my choice. People shift to places of their imagination. They give a repetitive pattern to their lives, let boredom set in, leading to discontent. The gap between their expectation and veracity increases. They complain, stay with melancholy, migrate to a distant land, or drift from one place to another seeking the right one. This is a reflection of their inner turmoil; dissatisfaction reigns in their lives in whatever they do. They are never at peace with themselves or others. They create mayhem wherever they go. They are critical about themselves, all the people they meet, and everything around them. This is disparaging, not prolific, for the society at large. A serene person carves the path of progress and evolution. I would not have fit into the frame of a composed and unruffled being. I have undergone a series of transformations to be the current Shalinii.

Raj and Vishal call me up when they reach home. I speak to Vidya and get connected to most of my friends through Facebook and WhatsApp. Technology has brought the world very close. I am talking and chatting with Simran in Dubai, Smriti in Canada, Poonam in Australia, or Anil in USA. None of these people want to know about Pawan or our divorce. Maybe they have been prewarned by Raj and Vidya. We hook up like old times. We form groups, remember, greet, and wish good luck to each other on birthdays and special events. It is like physically being with the others. It is the best part of my life. I am no more isolated from friends and family. I can access the latest treatment regimen at the click of a button. Photographs bring us closer to the days we spent together. Receding hairlines, excess weight, some wrinkles on the face here and there are our current characteristics. We exchange notes on patients, share the present good and bad times on a daily basis. I feel as if I am living in a dream.

I do miss Pawan, more so as I am within reach of most people of those times. I have no idea Raj and Vishal could speak to him or not. They do not converse about Pawan. I cannot gather enough courage to talk to them about him.

I assume that they would communicate to me if they learn his whereabouts. I expect them to pass on any information about Pawan, they lay their hand on, to me. I take it for granted that Pawan must not have talked to them. They have him wiped off as if he does not exist, which makes me anxious. I start to wonder if he is fine or not. I go through a suffocating feeling. I neither can talk about him nor can I keep quiet and watch each moment passing by. I only own my thought process at present. I take refuge in God and pray for Pawan's safety and well-being. I am dying to see Pawan.

CHAPTER THIRTEEN

I am sitting in my OPD attending medical representatives calls one day. Prashant, my junior assistant, comes in my room and informs me, 'There is a paediatric conference in Mumbai in a week, madam. Are you going for it?'

'Do you want to go, Prashant? You can go if you want to,' I tell him.

'No, madam, I will not be able to go. I have my sister's wedding after a month, and I have to make arrangements for it. I want to go for the next conference which is in November at Delhi. Why don't you go for this one along with Shasha? I and Amit will go for the next.'

'Speak to Shasha. If she wants to go, register our names and book the tickets.' I say this with the thought of meeting Vidya and her kids in Mumbai.

As I imagine myself going to Mumbai after so many years, I get nostalgic and happy. I am doing my routine work at present, visualizing the future makes my day today. This is what happens when we plan our life in advance. We do not leave anything to chance. It is up to us to achieve our targets, keeping in mind the pitfalls that may occur and some space for a likely breakdown. I am training myself to approach a well-sketched tomorrow.

Shasha wants to go to Mumbai. She has been educated in a local medical college at Nandurbar. Shasha is a young girl of twenty-five years who is eager to go to Mumbai as she has never been there before. We board a luxury bus for Mumbai on the day prior to the conference. We have a pleasant journey in the comfortable bus unlike the days of my MBBS. We reach Mumbai the next morning. Shasha wants to get a feel of the famous local trains of Mumbai, so I give up the thought of reaching the Hotel Taj Lands End, the place the conference is to be held, by taxi. Since we are to take a train against the direction of the rush hour crowd, we manage not only to get inside the train easily but also get place to sit. There are not many women in the ladies compartment that we are seated in. After two stations, small children get in as vendors selling eatables, stationary, and vegetables. The silence of the place is gone with their bustle. A teenage blind girl comes in at the next station with a child less than six months old. She is singing Hindi movie songs at the top of her voice. It has a sweet melody with an overture of sadness and grief reflecting her torturous young life. Shasha is moved by the sight and has tears in her eyes. She stretches her hand to reach out for her purse and withdraw money from it. I infer from her gesture what she is up to, hold her hand and signal her with my eyes to refrain from giving money to the girl. I so well remember a similar experience I have been through, years ago, when I was new to this wonder city.

'Do not encourage begging. It is an organized crime and a thriving business here. People are handicapped intentionally to get sympathy and alms. You cannot empathize with criminals who have created these downtrodden beings. I always tell you all to have a purpose to your life. It is for a reason. You can constructively do something for people like these if you have good will in your heart. The need of the time for India with the label of a developing country after so many years of independence is a revolutionary change in the mindset of its people. I have many doctors from my college who have migrated to the west because they are not valued enough in this place and the quality of life there, is far better than here. I dream of India being at par with them in a few years which is possible with consistent and dedicated effort by a bunch of truly motivated people.'

Shasha is moved by the hutments along the railway tracks. She cannot come to terms with the dirt and filth around these areas. 'Is this the city of Mumbai, I have heard so much about?' I could see the mirror image of a teenaged Shalinii in Shasha at this point in time.

'Shasha, the city of Mumbai is all this and much more. Above everything else is its free spirit and liveliness. It gives you a feeling of being alive and vibrant in the worst of situations. It has a charm of its own. You can enjoy life here whether you earn five hundred rupees a day or add as many zeros to it as you want. Everyone finds bread and butter in Mumbai even with just the basic qualification of being a human being.'

We check in at the hotel and get ready for the day, the day of reunions and academic excellence. Poorvi from my class is also a paediatrician and is going to be attending the conference with us. Vidya would be joining us for lunch which we plan to have at a separate venue than the conference as we wish to spend some quality time together, of course minus Shasha. I would be wearing a western outfit after many years. The Punjabi suit, which is a replacement of the traditional sari of the previous generations, has been my trademark for the past few years. We have been revolutionary in breaking the genre of the Indian sari existing since many years. It is not that the sari has lost its appeal; our fascination for comfort has taken us beyond it.

As I get dressed up, I start to put on some jewellery. My parents have given me a lot of gold and diamond earrings and necklaces as customarily given by all Indian parents to their daughters at the time of their marriage. It is analogous to a safe deposit vault, supposed to be the last resort the girl is to use to sustain her when faced with financially broke situations specifically when the husband is not willing to be responsible for her welfare. I reflect on that aspect of the use of gold and the meaning that is attached to the selling of this metal. It is the selling of a woman's precious asset. The value systems that we have had, have been brilliant. There is a need to change certain outlooks with the changing epoch. This was when women were not educated. My jewellery adorns the lockers of my banks most of the time. It is with me once in five to seven years. It is a strain on the economy of the country. The wealth in the form of gold is unutilized with no worth. It is an investment which is blocked and is not available for turnover on a day-to-day basis.

I look at the image in the mirror with appraisal and am pleased at the way I am presenting myself to my colleagues. Shasha is stunned at my renewed appearance.

'I have never seen you like this before, madam. Why don't you pay some attention to yourself?'

'That is the place of my work. I have a certain image there. People expect me to be in a certain way. I am fixed in that frame of a professional. It is not possible for me to break that mould people have got used to seeing me in.' The little voice in my head tells me, 'You do not do it because you feel "Whom should I do it for?" If Pawan would have been with you, you would have had to fit in the image of a lover and then you would have bothered to dress up well and apply make-up.' I calm the little voice with a shut up order from my brain.

'Do images really matter, madam?' Shasha's query is thought-provoking, and I utter the next sentence after a hiatus.

'You are right, Shasha, we form images, metaphors, similes, and restrict the personality of a person. There is loss of freedom, loss of liberty of self-expression, as if bound by chains from all sides. A person with no image is free, free to be any which way he wants to be. He does not have to wear a mask all day long. A person has to rise above his expected image, be strong to face the criticism and wrath of the society. It requires him or her to be liberated of their particular image in their own minds. What all great people like saints, freedom fighters, revolutionaries, great painters, and artists do, is the breaking of this image illusion. Unless this is broken, no creativity is possible. If a person's hands and legs are tied with a rope, how can he eat, drink, and make merry even when the best of food is served to him?'

We enter the first lecture hall where they are discussing neonatology, the facet of paediatrics I love. The topic is neonatal neurosurgery and its recent advances. It is delighting to know that the babies, who were aborted by obstetricians previously as they were not compatible with life, can now be saved with minimally invasive surgeries and have good prospects of living a healthy life. Certain lectures are monotonous with nothing new to learn and some are real eye-openers. I am longing to meet my friends. Th last lecture of the session begins. It is about some statistics in paediatrics. There is movement in the hall. People walk out as they are hungry and uninterested in the topic. I spot Poorvi sitting two rows ahead of me easily in the now sparsely populated hall. Shasha has made friends with a lone girl of her age from Solapur and is at ease in her company. I ask the two to be together, and I promise to meet them after lunch. I toddle down to where Poorvi is sitting and occupy the empty seat next to her. Poorvi is busy listening to the lecture when I interrupt her with a whisper.

'Hi. How's life?' I tap her on her shoulder, and she is startled. She smiles, and there is a bright twinkle in her eye on seeing me.

'Oh! Shalinii, at last I could meet you, and it's so nice to see you. I am fine, but you look the same, gorgeous and young,' she whispers back.

'Let's move out. Vidya must be waiting for us. This lecture should have been over by now. They aren't following the timeline properly,' I complain as we get up and slowly go out of the door carefully from the darkness in the hall, made for reading slides projected on the screen, into the bright light outside. We blink our eyes, and before we open them to see clearly in front of us, I hear Vidya calling.

'Shalinii!' she shouts loudly for all those present in the hallway to turn their heads and glance at us. I signal her to be silent as we reach her. We hug each other and remain like that for quite some time, not being bothered by our surroundings or people watching us.

'Vidya, you have become double your previous size. Start exercising immediately, dear mummy, pay attention to yourself. How are your kids? I want to meet them,' I cry out elated.

'You, Shalinii, have maintained the same statistics, is it not 36-26-36, am I right? Shalinii, we missed you so much. I and Raj were not getting married without the two of you. It was good we did not wait, otherwise we would have got married at an old age. People would have wondered whether it is our first or second marriage, and when do you think we would have had children?' Once she starts talking, Vidya continues like a superfast mail, non-stop. A person is never bored in her company that is the best part of her nature.

'We will go to the cafeteria on the first floor. They have good non-vegetarian food there.' Poorvi suggests. Vidya and I spontaneously accept her proposal.

We are seated, and Poorvi starts going through the menu card. Vidya realizes something and wants to get up and go out. I know what's going on in her mind.

'Vidya, please sit down. I will eat my much loved club sandwich.' Vidya takes her seat back on my insistence. Poorvi is looking from one to the other of us and does not understand what we are talking.

'I stopped eating non-vegetarian food since the time I am with Pawan as he is a pure vegetarian. His parents followed a particular religious sect which forbade non-vegetarian food. I still do not eat it. Vidya is concerned what I would eat,' I clarify for Poorvi's sake.

'Oh! I did not know!' Poorvi exclaims.

'Poorvi, being with each other is more important than eating food. I do not get to eat sandwiches in Dhadgaon.'

'How did you select that place, Shalinii?' quizzes Vidya.

'I was undecided about the place I wanted to stay in. As per my principles, I was to be where I was needed. My maternal aunt's son did his MBBS at Nandurbar and was posted on deputation at Dhadgaon during the monsoons. He had come to meet me and was describing how difficult survival was in this part of our state. I took a bus from my mom's place in Nashik to go to this place the next day morning. You know me well, I liked the place and went back with bag and baggage within a week and am there since then,' I enlighten them.

We make small talk; each of us behaves with the other like old times. We are laughing, joking, and making fun as if we are some teenagers in their own world. It is time for me and Poorvi to go back for the lectures.

'Shalinii, you are not staying in the hotel. Raj will come to take you home at night. You have to come and stay at my place,' Vidya announces this before departing.

'Vidya, I have a young girl with me whose responsibility solely lies on me. Excuse me today. I shall be at your house tomorrow by 4 p.m.'

'What is the point? You are to leave at 10 p.m. I had planned to be up the whole night with you,' Vidya says with such an ardour I do not have the heart to forfend her.

'Vidya, there is the banquet tonight. I do not want to attend it. But Shasha wants to, and I cannot leave her alone. Let us meet tomorrow, please. I would have invited you over, but I know Raj will not be able to manage the kids alone.' I do not want to act as an encumbrance on their daily routine work.

'Okay. As you wish. Do you ever listen to anybody? You will always do what you want to do.'

'That is because I do the right things. Don't you accept that?'

'Nobody has been able to win a debate with you and nobody can in future. Bye, see you tomorrow.'

'Bye, Vidya,' Poorvi and I echo together as we leave Vidya to rejoin the conference.

Teatime comes up fast as the paper presentations on various topics proceed quickly. There is the banquet at 9 p.m. As I have not slept well the previous night, I go to the room to have a small nap. Shasha wants to go for shopping with her newfound friend after the remaining lectures. Poorvi has her daughters to take care of, and she goes home, not planning to attend the banquet.

When I wake up, Shasha is busy putting make-up on her face, and she is almost ready for the celebrations.

'Madam, please wake up. It's time for us to go,' she says as soon as she sees me open my eyes.

'Shasha, you go ahead, I shall join you in some time. Is your friend going to be with you?'

'Yes, madam, but I want you to come. I will come back to the room if you do not come there in half an hour,' she threatens before leaving the room.

I want to refrain from the limelight. I keep reflecting on the days I have spent with Pawan. At such times, he would pull me along and make me dance with him till the wee hours of the morning. We would be the last ones to leave the hall. I do not know from where he would get so much energy. Initially, he would drink wine or vodka; later on slowly I made him give up any form of alcohol completely. I am neither awake nor asleep. I am visualizing him around me, talking and smiling as in the past. The alarm that I

Dr. Shital Vinay Patil

have set before sleeping in my mobile phone rings, making
me aware that it is 9 p.m. I have to give up my laziness and
get ready lest I mess up with Shasha's evening. I get up very
slowly and go to the washroom. I am ready in about half
an hour's time, during which I answer at least a dozen of
Shasha's calls. I am so overwhelmed by Pawan's thoughts
that I wear a suit presented by him on our last marriage
anniversary together in Chicago.

I walk down the winding spiral staircase to reach the
banquet hall. I enter inside to find unknown people. There
are more of men and hardly any women. 'My conference
has lots of women,' I almost say aloud. Where am I? I
wonder. All of a sudden, I spot a group of men chattering
with cigarettes and alcohol glasses in hand, smoking and
drinking away to glory. I see Pawan among those men. Our
eyes meet for a split second before he looks away. There is
no sign of recognition on his face or the slightest hint of
familiarity. I blink my eyes and pinch myself to be sure that
I am not daydreaming. I look again in the direction that I
saw him, and he is not to be seen. Where did he peter out
in a second? I do not know. How can it be him? He is not
in India. He has gone on some vacation. Could he have
come to India for a holiday? Was it him or somebody else I
mistook to be him?

I go out of the hall, looking for him all over the place.
Outside the hall is a display board which reads Urology
International Conference. I am sure I have seen him. I am
not imagining him to be there. What a rare coincidence it
is? We have our conferences in the same hotel. What do I
do? Whom do I ask? What if it is not him? My mind is up
to its games. I go inside again and look carefully all over

the place. I go up to the men and enquire about him, but they say they do not know where he is. I go to the hotel reception to find if he is staying in the hotel itself. 'Personal information about any of our customers cannot be divulged, madam' is the reply I get.

I have to take some help. I decide to trace him. I want to meet him. I call up Raj. His phone is engaged. I call up Vidya, and I start to talk as soon as she picks up the phone.

'Vidya, this is Shalinii, please give the phone to Raj.'

'Shalinii, what is the matter? Why are you screaming? Raj has not yet returned home. He is in the hospital.'

'Can you give me the landline number of the hospital? Okay. Wait, hold on, I think Raj is calling me up. I need to talk to him. I shall talk to you later on, bye, Vidya.' I put her off and find Raj's missed call. I call him back and his phone is engaged again. 'Oh! Whom is this man talking to again and again?' I almost cry out loudly. The receptionist is alarmed seeing my commotion; she enquires politely, 'Is something the matter, madam? Can I help you?'

'No, thank you' is all I manage to mutter, and I go and drop myself in one of the empty chairs in the hotel lobby, contemplating my next move. My phone starts ringing, and I am sure it is Raj.

'Shalinii, I am coming there immediately. Just calm down and wait for me. We will sort out whatever it is. I am with you always, don't worry. Vidya informed me.'

'Fine, I am at the reception.' I cut off the phone saying this. Vidya could palpate the alarm in my voice, and she conveyed it to Raj and he is on his way; this is enough for me to relax at present. The concerned receptionist has ordered a glass of fresh pineapple juice for me, handed over to me by the waiter, which I drink immediately. They are both surprised by the speed with which I empty the glass and hand it over. In comes Raj with an apprehensive look.

'What is the matter, Shalinii?' he queries.

'Raj, I have seen Pawan here some time back. He disappeared into thin air as if by magic.'

'Shalinii, do you think you need to consult a psychiatrist?'

'Raj, what are you saying? I swear, I have seen him here today.'

'I accept you saw him. I shall go and search for him. Meanwhile, you go join your party.' I want to go with Raj. I am conscious of Shasha's multiple phone calls and am sure she must have been out of her mind by now. There is no option for me but to go and find her.

'Very well, Raj, you find him and meet me. I am in room number 304 on the second floor.' I run upstairs to the correct hall this time. I have a quiet dinner in the form of fruits and am away from the merriment, with Shasha and a few colleagues, while awaiting Raj and Pawan's return. Raj returns in another half an hour.

'Shalinii, I have tried to search for him. I could not find him. I called him up, and he is on duty, at his workplace in Chicago. Please calm down and come with me to our house.'

'No, Raj, thank you. I shall go and sleep. I think I am tired. I am fine, don't worry.' I say this with incertitude and go to my room quickly without giving him a chance to say anything. I do not want to talk to anyone, and I want to return to the secure atmosphere of my house at the earliest.

It is one of the darkest nights of my life where sleep is not ready to befriend me. I spend the night in the balcony of the hotel room for two reasons: I do not wish to wake

Shasha up and I need some fresh air to be alive. At dawn, I shiver and enter the soft unused bed. I am woken up for lunch by Shasha the next afternoon. I have a terrible headache. I push some food down my gullet, call Vidya to apologize. She understands my plight, is okay with me not going to her house. I run away from the city close to my heart, Mumbai, within forty-eight hours of being in it. I am running from the love of my life as well. Is it a pattern of my life to run away from places, people, and things that do not need me, rather I feel they do not need me? I got what I asked for. I wanted to meet Pawan but was apprehensive, and so he evaporated. I have these thoughts when I board the bus at 5 p.m.—five hours in advance of my schedule to return home.

In the bus, Shasha has many queries. 'Madam, why do most of the male doctors drink and smoke? They know the ill effects of the two vices, don't they? I mean, it is fine with the rest of the professionals like engineers or architects or lawyers or businessmen, but why doctors? We see so many patients with terminal liver damage due to chronic alcoholism or nicotine-related cancer of the mouth, the lung damage, etc. Are they not scared to have the same problems themselves?'

'Shasha, first of all doctors too are human beings with the same pitfalls as any other person. It starts very early in life for them. They succumb to the pressures of the education system. Most of us then have been from middle- or even lower-middle-class families. The stress of the exams, the future which seems in the darkness then, family strain, self-doubt, anxiety to pass through the grind of the medical studies, and getting postgraduation in the subject of one's choice, later on having a hospital of our own with the meagre financial backing from the family, puts them at a high risk of addictions at an early age, right inside the medical campus itself. I am not justifying it. We also have gone through all this. But there always is a difference. Women usually would get married and settle down. The onus of the planning for the future usually lies with the men, was a dictum of the past generations.

'Times are changing now. Not that women were less ambitious, but the way the society was then, bread earning was more of a man's job. People were less liberal in their thoughts. The reason for the generation gap is because of this. The previous generations had more of housewives. Well-educated women were also not allowed to work. Education was sort of just to procure educated husbands. With the liberalization of the society, the roles of men and women changed. The increase in the number of divorces is because of this reason. Men who have seen their mothers managing the households and families fully without any support from their husbands find it difficult to have women earning and asking for equality with them in all respects. It is not the fault of these men.

'What you saw at the conference was people drinking and getting drunk. How often a practicing consultant who has to tend to emergencies can get drunk on a regular basis? It is not possible as he has to attend to emergency patients at any time of the day or night. These are places where he can shed his inhibitions with his peers and enjoy. Such times are once or twice in a year for him. He is going to take advantage of it. Doctors are not gods, though they have a respectable image to maintain. How many times it is so, that we know certain things, we have knowledge which we do not apply practically. I would give you an example: there are many obese people who know what they are supposed to eat, the daily exercise that they are supposed to do. They want to be fit and healthy, but they are not. Maybe some of them can write a book on health and fitness. This is human nature, and these are human tendencies.

'The society is made up of individuals, by and large, an individual is a reflection of the society and the society a reflection of individual people. Any wrongdoing in the society is not because of a handful of people. It shows the general consensus of the society. For example, if rapes are committed in our society, who is to be blamed? The rapist? No, not just them, it is all of us. We tolerate them. We give such an environment to our children that they transform into rapists and criminals. The context of life he sees and interprets or misinterprets makes a person whatever he is.'

CHAPTER FOURTEEN

The backlog of work back home does not give me time to ponder on the proceedings of the past few days. I am in touch with all my friends in the same way I was prior to going to Mumbai. I try to flush the fact that I saw Pawan, out of my system. I take it for granted that it was a mistake on my part, though my brain does not admit it.

About a week after my return, I receive a registered letter which is not in my maiden name. The name on it is Mrs Shalinii Mallik with my complete residential address. I open it with trembling hands to find the divorce papers I had signed earlier at the time when I left Chicago. I recognize the papers and my signature. I had not read those papers in detail then and do not want to go through them now. I put the bundle away into the safe compartment of my cupboard where I keep all my valuable documents. At one instance, I feel like throwing it into the dustbin. Why have these papers been sent to me? I do not comprehend.

'I am not going to attach any meaning or significance to this recent development,' I say aloud twice to fix it in my head. 'No thinking and no prejudices or expectations, give up all the stories I would be creating around those pieces of paper,' I warn myself and help myself forget the document for my own sake.

The next two months have been very eventful. The plan of the new hospital and the surrounding area has been sanctioned and is ready to be implemented. Mr Ramdas has won the elections. He and his son have new wives, and I am happy for them. Shasha has got engaged to the brother of the friend she met during the conference, who is an anaesthetist. He visits Dhadgaon and plans to stay here. I get an additional doctor's hand for my projects. Vidya's son is in the tenth grade, and he has his board exams, and she is busy with his studies. So are most of my friends with children in higher classes. They are reviving their teens with their children.

I receive a call from Vishal on a Monday, early in the morning. When the phone rings, I am not even fully awake.

'Hello!'

'Hello! This is Shalinii speaking.'

'Shalinii, Vishal here.'

'Yes, Vishal, how are you?'

'Shalinii, I am fine. I called up to remind you about our get together.'

'Yes, I am aware, Vishal, that it is on coming Saturday. Have you sent invitations to all the people? How are the preparations going on?'

'Everything has been done. I have sent invitations to all those people whose address and phone numbers I could lay my hands on. I shall come to fetch you at your place. We are to meet at 8 a.m. in the college canteen on Saturday, the 30th of December.'

'Vishal, I have a lot of things lined up to be done on coming Sunday. Will it do if I do not come? As it is I am in touch with most of you on the phone. Who all are coming?'

'Shalinii, I am done with you and your stupid reasons. Keep them to yourself. I am coming to take you and that is it. A hundred and fifty of us have confirmed and are expected to be there.'

'Vishal, is Pawan coming?' I could not prevent myself from asking that question.

'Raj is in touch with him. He has some issues regarding getting leave from his workplace. He was recently on a vacation, soliciting a leave of absence within a few days of it, is not going to be feasible for him. He is trying his best to be present for the get together.'

'Vishal, that means you all could at least communicate with him. How is he?' I cannot hide my exhilaration.

'Shalinii, I have spoken to him once. He is fine. Raj is coordinating with him for our gathering on Saturday. I shall be at your place by Friday afternoon. Gear up and prepare yourself from today itself.'

'I shall do that, Vishal. Thank you and bye.'

I want to meet all my dear friends. I want to meet Pawan. I do not want to go there with the expectation that I shall be able to meet him. If he cannot manage to come, the disappointment that I would face is something I do not want to experience. It is better to keep my fingers crossed and pray to God that he better come to India. But if he is not there, I have to be all right with it for the sake of the others. I should not be spoiling the atmosphere and party mode of the rest of my friends.

I start to pack up my bags in advance for the first time in my life, paying heed to the details of how to dress up, what footwear to use, and what accessories to pack. This is going to be a major occasion for me to celebrate in my otherwise routine days. I must not have groomed myself to this extent when I got married. People working with me start to notice the difference in my way of being. Ruby casually comments, 'Madam, is your husband coming to India?'

To this I simply say, 'I do not know, Ruby. I am going to meet up some of my old friends over the weekend. I hope to be back by Monday. In case I am not back, I shall convey to you and you distribute my patients to the others.' I have made a hierarchy at my workplace. In my absence, things are going to be handled by efficient contemporaries.

Friday arrives and I cannot contain my happiness. I work up to lunch hour, complete giving some last moment directions to my staff, and then I proceed to my house. I await the arrival of Vishal. I do not call him up or the others. I do not want to bother Raj and Vidya. They must have been too busy making all the arrangements. It is not a joke to arrange the accommodation and food for 150 odd people coming from all the corners of the globe. Calling up Vishal at this instance would burden him while driving. I have to kill time until he comes. It is 8 p.m. There is no sign of Vishal or his message. Did he play a prank on me? Why would he do that? To see the way I would react to the trick? Have they collectively made a fool of me? I am becoming restless. I start to pace aimlessly in my hall. People are in the habit of making promises and not keeping them. Raj and Vishal were not on time when they were here to see me a few months back. A person who does not honour his word and does not communicate or convey has a negative impression on people's mind. I am in the dark at this instant. I am fatigued, the exhaustion of always waiting for someone.

I wake up to the ringing of the doorbell. I check the clock as I go to open the door. It is 10 p.m.

'Raj, how come you are here? Where's Vishal? I hope he is fine.' I start to talk as I see Raj instead of Vishal in front of me.

'Shalinii, why do you always have to go into pessimism? Vishal was receiving our friends at the airport, so I replaced him. Give me a glass of water, and where are your bags? We will have to leave immediately.'

'Raj, we will not be able to drive down the ghats in the dark. This is a hilly area. The condition of the roads is not good. You will have to drive all night to reach in the morning. I could have come by bus. I am sorry you have to take so much trouble for me.'

'Shut up, Shalinii, I came because you would not have come. Give me your bags and your party time starts now. Enjoy the ride with me. When otherwise would you have been in my company alone?' By the time I go to fetch water for him, he keeps my bags in the car. I lock the door of my house, and we are seated in the car.

'Raj, did you have your dinner? You must be worn out by the ride. Do you want to take some rest?'

'Shalinii, I am all right and energized with the thought of meeting old buddies. I am not hungry. I had grub on the way while coming here. We should be leaving immediately if we are to reach on time. It is going to be a privilege for me to be with you for the whole night.' He laughs aloud.

'Raj, are you going to flirt with me all along the way?'

'Do you think I would miss the opportunity?' Raj winks at me, smiles, and further adds lest I become uncomfortable, 'Shalinii, don't you have faith in me? And you know me well. I am no more the young Raj madly in love with you. I have a beautiful wife, and I love her. I am a father of two wonderful kids. I would not flirt with my wife's best friend and the wife of my best pal.' He utters this and bites his own tongue. I do not mind him saying this as it is true; somewhere although I am divorced on paper, I do consider myself to be Pawan's wife.

Raj is lost in some thought and misses a turn. He is about to bump into a tree but puts on an emergency brake at the last moment. The car is not at a high speed preventing a major catastrophe.

'Are you sleepy, Raj? We could have had a cup of coffee at my place before starting.'

'No, Shalinii, I am not sleepy. I am contemplating whether to ask you a question or not?'

'Raj, you can ask me whatever you want to if it is troubling you.'

Raj slows down the car until it comes to a halt on a sideway on the road. He turns to face me and looks into my eyes as if trying to search for something there.

'Shalinii, did you ever even for a split second love me?'

I smile before answering him, 'Why should that make a difference to you?'

'It does not affect me, but the feeling I get is of having loved and lost which is difficult to bear.'

'Don't you love Vidya, and does she not love you?'

'Vidya loves me more than anybody can love any other person on this earth, and I too cannot stay alive without her.'

'Why then do you need my approval for you to feel complete about yourself?'

'Somewhere deep within me I feel incomplete and a failure. I cannot accept the fact that Vidya loves me though

I know it to be true. I feel as if I am not worth loving because you rejected me. It gives me a pain in the heart at all times.'

'Raj, you are being emotional now. What has the heart got to do with this pain? It is your view of looking at things. *Rejection* and *failure* are words coined by you in reference to yourself for the fact that I did not reciprocate your love. I love the sun. Can I expect it to love me too? What do you mean by saying you loved and you lost? What did you lose? You lost your worth, your self-esteem, in whose eyes and whose mind, your own. Why are you using a past tense for your love? Is it over or empty? Love is eternal, if you say you love me, you should still love me as a good friend.

'Love has various forms. If I love Pawan as my husband, I do love you as a friend. It is not as though I preferred Pawan over you. There are no predilections as far as loving a person is concerned. I love you very much, if my saying this gives you satisfaction. I love you, the only divergence is that I have never had and will not ever have sex with you, in case you consider that as love. Otherwise I have as much love and respect for you as a person as I do for Pawan. I was always physically attracted to Pawan for some unknown reason. But that is not the only reason I married him and not you. When you proposed marriage to me, I was not willing to give marriage a thought. Things were altogether altered when Pawan proposed to me. I had gone through a life-threatening incidence, and I valued the need for a companion in my life. I had no fear until then and did not feel it necessary to have a life partner. You are a buddy close to me and shall remain so. It is my failure to have missed on you as my lover. But that is not my way of looking at it. I consider myself blessed to have both of you in my life. For that matter, I am privileged to have a flock of good people in my life. You do not need my confession that I love and respect you. You should have realized it from my actions.'

'Shalinii, you make things look simpler.'

'Life is simple, you complicate it by your qualms.'

Raj is an efficient driver. He manoeuvres well through the narrow, steeply down going curvy roads. He is cheery now. We are listening to music and chit-chatting along the way. He tells me who all are coming for the get together. He provides me with the details of who is doing what, married to whom, and where each one is settled. He is keeping a secret from me though. He isn't making any comment on Pawan's status of coming to India. I feel as if he is teasing me by talking about everything under the sun but about the person I want to hear about. I decide not to ask him. I am silent about Pawan for some time. But I end up asking him.

'Raj, is Pawan coming.'

'No, Shalinii, he could not make it. He will be coming next year. He plans to meet you. He said we will have a get together at Dhadgaon when he comes.' He speaks without blinking an eyelid. I on my part hide my disappointment by yawning and pretending to be very sleepy. At least he has bothered to ask about me and wants to meet me. I do not say a word after that and am asleep, waking up in between small intervals of time to make sure Raj is awake. Raj, on his part, concentrates on driving. He has to be careful due to the oddity of the hour, length of the distance to be travelled, and within a record time as we have to reach early.

I am being woken up by Vidya. I am in the car in her driveway. The watch shows it to be 5.30 a.m. I rest for a while before breakfast and a bath at her house. I am about to dress up for the occasion when I hear Vidya saying something that bowls me over.

'There is a dress code, Shalinii.'

'What is it?'

'All women are to be in saris and all men in suit and tie.'

'Vidya, I do not have a sari, that means I cannot come. Why did you not convey this to me before?'

'Don't you worry. I have got the right sari for you. I have bought it for you and stitched a blouse too.'

'Where did you get the measurements from?'

'Do you remember I had taken one of your marriage saris which I had liked along with the blouse? I had it, and I gave it to the tailor for your measurements. You have not changed since that time.'

'I do not know how to wear it, and it might come off. I am not used to wearing saris. Do you remember on one of our sari day in college, my sari had come off and a patient in the side room of the ward helped me put it back in place?'

'I have answers for that. I will put it on for you and pin it up in such a way that you do not have to worry.'

'Whose idea was it about this funny dress code?'

'Why do you find it funny? Dear, this is the tradition of our country. I cannot tell you who suggested this dress code.'

'Why can you not tell me? It must be that stupid Vishal. He has not got married himself, what does he know about women?'

'No, it is not him. Do you have any idea why he is not married?' We are gossiping as old times while Vidya puts the sari on me, carefully pinning it at every possible angle to fix it properly in place.

'Why did he not get married?'

'Do you know he had tuberculosis during our college days?'

'Yes, I know.'

'Well, what you do not know is that he was diagnosed with HIV also.'

'What, what are you talking about, Vidya?' I almost screech which sounds too loud as against Vidya's whispers.

'Yes, it seems there was a diabetic patient with HIV in the medical ward whose HIV status he was not aware of, in fact nobody was aware of at that time. Vishal would do the bedside blood sugar of this patient four to five times in a day. He would love to do it. Once he pricked himself with the used needle of the patient accidentally, which had lots of blood in it. It was a deep injury. He was doing the tests without using gloves, and he also had another deep cut wound on his hand. Infected blood spilled more than twice on his open wound. Later on, when the patient was to undergo surgical intervention for his diabetic foot, his HIV test was done and the result was positive. Vishal did his test some months later which tested positive. He is on ART and his CD 4 counts are low.'

'Who told you all this? My god! Really bad! He has sacrificed himself because of a silly mistake and this profession. This could have happened to any of us. He has been the unfortunate guy. He is one of the most caring friends I have, and my respect for him has multiplied many folds after hearing this. He is suffering unnecessarily.'

'Obviously Raj told me this long after we got married. He and Pawan knew it all along. They have always been his best friends.'

Raj's parents are to stay with the children so as to allow the couple to enjoy their days off. We go out of her house with our bags as the arrangement for us to stay has been made someplace else. I have not been taken into confidence, and the whole plan of the weekend has not been revealed to me. I do not mind not knowing since I am here with my friends; wherever it is they take me, I am going to enjoy.

We reach the campus or rather our campus; it is ours because we still have the memoirs of this place fresh in our minds. There is a flooding of the canteen and its surrounding area, the so-called Kutta in those days, with 150 odd fortyish middle aged folks in suits, ties, and saris, colourful attires resembling a corporate meet, unseen of on medical campuses. My eyes are scanning the place with an X-ray vision to detect the man of my interest. I see him seated on the library staircase book in hand as he used to be seated in the past. He is the same as I had left him ten years ago.

'Wait a minute, Shalinii, you may be daydreaming again,' I tell myself, I am being reminiscent. 'I am not making a fool of myself again.' I decide and put my head down and avoid looking in his direction. I am talking and meeting many old friends with an eye on him. He is busy chit-chatting with Vishal. I keep looking at him once in a while from the corner of my eye, and he is still there.

'Are you angry with me? I have been watching you since some time, and I thought you would come and talk to me. I smiled at you twice when I thought you were looking at me. You did not respond. You do not want to recognize me or you did not actually recognize me? What is it, Shalinii?' Pawan comes from behind me and says all this in an instant.

I keep staring at him without saying a word. He waves his hand in front of my eyes and says, 'Hello, are you sleeping with open eyes? What is wrong with you? I am not a ghost.' I still do not react. I am too stunned to say anything. The lack of sleep from the day before, the overtiredness due to travelling, lowered blood sugar level having not eaten much in the past twenty hours, and Pawan's sudden appearance make me feel giddy, and I start perspiring. I feel nauseated, and I sit down on a nearby chair. Pawan is too much of a doctor not to notice I am hypoglycacmic, and hc knows of my irregular eating habits. He immediately gets a glass of cold lime juice with lots of sugar in it. I drink the juice as fast as possible. Vishal brings me idli and vada which I gobble in no time. I do not want to make an issue in front of everybody. I want to be fine soon to get out of the guilt that I get after seeing many anxious faces around me. I make an attempt to stand up as soon as I feel better, but I am weak still and I have to sit down again. I start talking to make myself and others feel that I am well.

'Thanks, Vishal, and thanks to you too.' I look at Vishal and then at Pawan to thank both of them.

'I do not like this formal behaviour, grandmother-style, and sacrificial attitude of yours. When was the last time you ate food?' Pawan demands.

'I am sorry,' I say meekly whereas what I want to say is 'It is none of your business whether I eat or not. I do not care what you like and what you do not like.'

There is the sun above my head where I am sitting. I get up and go and sit on the library kutta in the shade away from most people since I start getting an aura of a migraine attack. No sooner than I sit there, Vishal comes and sits beside me. We start to converse about the old canteen which has now been replaced by a new structure. In about another minute, Pawan joins us. Taking some clue from him, Vishal leaves the two of us alone.

'How are you feeling now?' Pawan asks gently.

'I am much better but looks like I would get migraine.'

'I too get it frequently these days. I keep this in my pocket.' He brings forth a tablet from the back pocket of his pants and hands it over to me and gets up and goes away. He returns with a glass of water in hand urging me to take the tablet. I swallow the tablet with a gulp of water from the glass.

'Shalinii, did you check what I just gave you. How could you eat stuff given to you randomly without checking the contents? I had sent a letter to you, the contents of which you did not bother to check.'

'I received the letter with the divorce papers in it. I recognized the brown envelope and the yellow paper so I did not go through the painful procedure of reading all the papers in detail.'

'You should have done that.'

'What difference would that have made?' I say to myself angrily while maintaining quiescence on the outside. We are both silent, and I start to think of something to keep the conversation going. People around are watching us.

'Have you come here alone or along with your wife?'

'Well, I am with my wife.'

'Where is she now? Has she gone for shopping, or have you left her alone in the hotel room?'

'My wife is always with me.' I could not understand head or tail of this statement. I want to know whether she is in India or not. His answer does not convey it to me. I do not want to know anything from him now. I make a dirty face and look at him.

'I mean in my heart,' he says and laughs aloud.

'Oh! She must be a lucky lady.'

'I do not know of that. I am lucky to have her as my wife.'

I am at the pinnacle of my endurance. I again have to think of turning this talk somewhere else. I am digging my own grave. The more I talk to the man in front of me, the deeper the grave is going to be. I look around for some clue to talk to him. Our friends are all gathering and having breakfast. There are some more of us to come, and we have to wait for them before the next program can be started. How I detest sitting here with the man I know not whether I love or hate more. I have no choice. Destiny has put us together along with many of our friends. We cannot be fighting or creating a scene in front of them.

'Are you going to leave immediately for Chicago, or do you plan to stay for few days?'

'That will depend on my wife's wishes. If she says so, I might not even go back,' he replies coolly. I could feel my heart pumping and my blood gushing forcefully in my veins.

'You do love your wife a lot, don't you?'

'Yes, I not only love her but respect her too. She is a real woman of substance.' I have tears welling up in my eyes. I abruptly go away from him with the excuse of going to the toilet before I break into a sob and make a fool of myself.

Vidya follows me to the washroom as she sees me running towards it. When I do not open the door for quite some time, she calls out my name from outside the washroom.

'Shalinii, have you finished? We need to go. Everybody is here.'

'Yes, Vidya, you go ahead, give me a sec, I shall be with you.'

I wipe off the tears, wash my face, and put on some face pack before opening the door. Vidya is standing there.

'What happened? Did you finally vomit?' she asks me with concern in her eyes.

'I am feeling better now,' I lie to her as we go and join the others.

CHAPTER FIFTEEN

We are to go to the MLT and interact with our teachers and students studying in the college at present. Some of our lecturers and professors who had retired have been specially invited. They are felicitated by us. They give short speeches. They talk of their experiences with the two to three batches of students of our times that are present in the hall. I am in awe of their memory. They remember the names of some of us. I try and stay as away from Pawan as possible, intermingling with the current students most of the time. I hear my name being called out on the mike. The organizer of the function, Vishal, is calling out my name. I do not know why I am being called on stage. I stand up not knowing what to do as I have been busy talking to a third-year student and am unaware of the context for me being called. Raj and Pawan come to escort me when I make no efforts to go on stage.

'Friends, we would like to felicitate a special lady present here amongst us,' Raj announces this as I am walking up the stairs leading to the stage. I notice Pawan walking beside me. I ignore him and look at Raj who continues.

'She stays in a rural area and has been working for the development and growth of the lives of the people of that area since the past ten years. I would request Dr Pawan to present her with a floral bouquet and a garland.' Pawan gives me the bouquet and puts the garland around my neck which

I remove and put aside. I see Vidya clicking our photographs. What is the use of these photos? This is going to be an additional memory of this college and my ex-husband for me to treasure. Thus I become a headliner of the reunion.

The program at the college ends, and we are to proceed to Hotel Delhi Darbar for lunch. I love the food at that hotel. I want to thank Vishal once again for choosing this place for lunch. Everyone enjoys the lunch. The next we are to go to The Renaissance to deposit our luggage, take some rest, freshen up with a high tea before going to a surprise venue. We would be spending the night at the next location and returning to the hotel in the morning for breakfast.

I put my bags in my room and go to Vidya's room. Raj is too tied up with making arrangements for us to go to the next site. I and Vidya have a nice time conversing about all the people.

'I wish Simran and Poonam could have come. We would have taken over this gathering and sent these men spinning away.'

'Shalinii, our husbands are a part of these men. Don't say such things.'

'Raj is your husband, Vidya. I have no husband.' I become serious all of a sudden.

'Shalinii, have you started to develop revulsion towards men?'

'No, not at all, Vidya. I am just pissed off because of Pawan. I cannot comprehend his feelings for me and my feelings towards him. I mean, I cannot stop loving him or hating him. Every single time I look at him, I love him more and then I cannot be with him. It is wrong for me to think of him. Why did you ask him to honour me on stage? It becomes very torturous for me to be in his company. Where are we going for the night? Can you ask Raj if I could stay in this hotel itself and see you all at breakfast? I am tired and am going to sleep.'

'Shalinii, it is not about Raj wanting you to come or not. All of us are to be together tonight. Vishal has done this as he is scared he would die soon. It is for him that you have to come. He would otherwise feel you did not like the venue and opted out of it. Please come, we will enjoy.'

'Where are we going?'

'That's a top secret. We will be moving in sometime, and you will see for yourself where we go.'

We take luxury buses after tea to reach our destination. There are four buses for us. I do not get into the one in which Pawan goes. Nobody knows where we are going except a select few. We cross the whole of Mumbai and are headed south towards the seashore. We get down at a shore and are asked to get into small motor boats. Vidya, Poorvi, Ragini, Anil, Sushant, and Raj are with me in the boat.

'Are we going on a cruise?' Poorvi queries Raj.

'Poorvi, you have guessed rightly.' This is Vidya's reply to her.

'That means we will be spending the night at the sea. I cannot come with you all. I shall get motion sickness.'

'Have you been on a cruise before?' Raj asks me.

'No, but I will not be able to tolerate being on the ship for long.'

'Shalinii, you go to a hotel, do you not? Imagine a hotel in the sea on a ship. Can you see that ship over there? That's our cruise liner. We will go from this boat to that one and be in it until morning.'

'Will it move?' I ask like a small child.

'No, it will not. It will stand where it is right now.'

'Oh! That's fine with me. We are not going deep into the sea, and Mumbai is close by, so if I have to come back, I can come in one of these small boats,' I say happily, feeling satisfied that I am not going to be in a danger zone. I see Vidya and Poorvi smiling at each other.

In the Starship, we are made to sit in one big hall. 'We will play some games,' announces the DJ. He explains us the rules of the game, and we start to play. It is a modification of dumb shards. We are sitting in a circle, half the circle is one team and the other half the other. Vidya and Poorvi are on one side of me and Raj, Pawan, and Vishal on the other side. Just as we start to play the game, there is the loud noise of the starting of an engine. I look from Vidya to Poorvi to Raj. The ship moves, and I hold Vidya's hand.

'You liar! you lied to me that this would not move, didn't you, Raj'

'You would not realize its motion in a few minutes. You will enjoy this journey,' Pawan says instead of Raj.

'Shalinii, you would not have come if we would have told you the truth.'

I keep quiet and try to concentrate on the game. We play for some time and go to the deck. The cool breeze there uplifts my senses, and I like the cruise. A Hindi movie song program starts on the deck, and we sit and enjoy the songs while eating hot snacks which are served to us. I am in a frivolous mood. I walk up and down the ship and even visit the captain's cabin. 'We are in international waters,' the captain informs me.

I go all around the place and am very happy to be there. We gather in the hall after some time, and there is music and dancing. I watch my friends dancing. Raj holds my hand and brings me into the dancing arena. Pawan too is on the dance floor. He is dancing in between his drinking spells with most other men. It's cold on the ship, and many women too have to resort to drinking wine to keep warm. The weather is chilly, and I start to feel very cold. I tug my shawl tightly around me. Pawan comes very close to me and urges me to take a sip of the forbidden liquid from his glass. 'You would not be able to tolerate the cold, Shalinii. Please have a few sips,' he says placidly, and his eyes look caringly at me as I refuse his offer.

There is deceleration in the motion of the ship, and I start to feel nauseated again, and as I am about to throw up, I rush to the washroom and I vomit. I have two or three bouts of vomiting after which I take a tablet to prevent motion sickness, and I go off to sleep in one of the cabins.

I wake up in the morning and am dozing off on the return journey. Back in the safety of the hotel room, I sleep comfortably. The phone in the room rings, and I pick it up half asleep.

'Hello, yes, who is it?' I ask as I pick up the receiver.

'Madam, can you give the phone to sir please? There is a call for him from Chicago.' The word *Chicago* rings a bell in my ears and I am wide awake.

'Whom is the phone for?' I ask.

'Madam, it is for your husband, Dr Pawan,' the lady on the other side answers back.

'Pawan is not in this room,' I say brusquely.

'Madam, but this room has been booked in the name of Mrs and Dr Pawan Mallik.'

'What, will you repeat what you just said,' I request her and I am out of the bed.

'Yes, madam, that is right, there is no mistake. I have double checked and the caller has also given me this room number.'

'Okay, put the call through to me,' I order her.

'Hello!' is all I say and wait for the other person to speak.

'Hello, Pawan, this is Dylan. Can you hear me?'

'Hello, Pawan is not here. Is there some message I can give him?'

'Is it Shalinii?'

'Yes, it is.'

'Shalinii, this is Dylan. I am Pawan's colleague. We have not met, but Pawan keeps talking about you, so it is as though I know you. When Pawan left Chicago he liquidated all his assets into cash and transferred it to your account in India, except for his house. He wrapped up from here, resigned his job, never to return. He had asked me to put his house on for auction since he did not have the time to do that. I did what he asked me to do. He has mailed me a few hours back asking me not to go ahead with the sale of his house and that he is returning in a few days. The house has already been transferred to its new owner, and I was about to send the money to India. What should I do?'

'Transfer the money. Are you his friend?' I ask her instead of 'Are you his wife?'

'Yes, I am his best friend and proud to be that. You have a wonderful husband, and he loves you so much. I am jealous of you.'

'Thank you and bye,' I say as quickly as possible. 'Bye' is all I hear as I put the receiver back.

I call up Vidya's room. Raj picks up the phone.

'Where is Pawan?' He realizes the urgency in my voice.

'He is in Vishal's room that is two rooms to the right of your room. What is the matter, Shalinii?'

I do not answer and run to the door in my nightdress with slippers. I hang on to my scepticism and do not want to pass on any information unless I preface it with my honest opinion. I press the doorbell of Vishal's room with all my might. I keep pressing it until an irritated Vishal opens the door.

'Is Pawan here?' I ask him, and I go inside the room without waiting for his reply.

Pawan is on the bed fast asleep. 'That is what I was about to tell you. He is sleeping.'

'Wake him up. I have got to talk to him urgently.'

Raj and Vidya enter Vishal's room. Raj repeats, 'Shalinii, can you tell me what is the matter?'

'I have to speak to him this moment,' I shout like a psychiatry patient, and Pawan wakes up.

I go and shake him up and shout again, 'What is all this about?'

'What are you asking me? I do not get you.' He is once again very calm and kind.

'I received a call from Dylan. Who is she, and what was she saying?'

'Did you speak to her? She is a friend. I have not spoken to her, so how do I know what she was saying?'

'You were planning to settle in India and then you decided against it, why?'

'Oh! She told you that?' He starts laughing and all of us look from one to the other.

'I told you, Shalinii, if my wife is fine with me staying here I would, but I do think she wants me to go, so I am going back.' Vidya, Raj, and Vishal smile at each other, and I feel as if all of them are conspiring against me. I am about to throw one more of my tantrums when Vishal interrupts.

'Why don't the two of you go to your room and sort out, I need to sleep, I am tired.'

I and Pawan go to my room, Vidya and Raj to theirs.

'Pawan, can you please tell me where your wife is?'

'She is with me.' He smiles again, and it annoys me more.

'Pawan, do not play games with me. Tell me where the hell is your wife.'

'Shalinii, did we not get married, so are you not my wife?'

'Pawan, where is your other wife?'

'I have only one wife, and that is you.'

'But we got divorced.'

'We never got divorced.'

'But the papers that I signed before leaving you?'

'They were property transfer papers. I transferred the house that I owned in Chandigarh in your name, and they were those papers which you signed. I sent them to you a few days back, but you did not even read them.'

'I am sorry.' It takes some time for the words that Pawan just said to percolate inside me. I keep looking at him sheepishly and with suspicion. 'You mean to say we are still husband and wife and not divorced?' He looks at me with love in his big black eyes and smiles approvingly. I hug him tightly and kiss him and then as an afterthought I ask him, 'Why did you send me away, and who was that lady you wanted to get married to?'

'There was no lady. I could not see you sitting in the house the whole day not doing anything. You were following my dreams. What about your aspirations? I wanted you to have your own separate identity, your individuality. I was killing you by keeping you there in the US with me. I told you so many times to go back. You would not listen, so I had to think of a way to send you to India. You loved me so much that you did not even verify the truth and did not check the documents. I could not leave my research incomplete. I have completed it. I am going to spend the rest of my life in the town that you have created. I would be more than happy to be recognized as your husband.'

'One last question, were you at the Taj Lands End hotel for the urology conference?'

He laughs aloud. 'Yes, I was there. I had not finalized my plans of coming to India at that time. I wanted to tell you the truth after being sure of coming back. I did not want you to come to me leaving your work incomplete here.'

'Pawan, you should not have done this. I was happy with you all along. Do not ever again leave me alone and go away. I have suffered a lot in the past ten years.'

'I am sorry, I am really sorry, Shalinii. You would never have realized what you are capable of. You would have remained in my shadow. I did not want you to be known as only Mrs Pawan Mallik.'

'Since when do Vishal and Raj know your secret?'

'Vishal could never digest that I would leave you for another woman. After he met you, he was sure of it. He spilled the beans on me instead of me telling him the truth. It was he who persuaded me to come back at the earliest. Raj and Vidya were told later on. In fact, I met Raj that night at Taj Lands End and told him everything. I knew you would not be convinced easily. I had to take him into confidence. Vidya was told when we planned the get together. We swore her to secrecy. Madam, I want to sleep, can we have this question and answer session some other time?'

'Yes, but you have not promised me certain things.'

'I will never ever leave you alone.'

'And what else?'

'The oath that I have to take about not touching alcohol again.'

'You have broken that promise.'

'There was nothing I could do to forget you, I missed you a lot. I had to resort to drinking alcohol to survive the cold too.'

'I also missed you, I did not start drinking alcohol.'

'You were in a hot country. I was in a cold one.'

'What has hot and cold to do with we not being together?'

'Do I need to tell you? I missed the warmth of your heart in a cold country.'

'Shut up, Pawan, and go to sleep.'

I fall asleep in no time in his warm embrace. I sleep peacefully after many years in his secure arms. We sleep all the way through the afternoon, and when we wake up, it is beginning to be dark outside. The reunion has come to its fag end. We are to have an early dinner and then say goodbye to each other.

We gather for the last supper of the gathering. I and Pawan mingle in the crowd together for the first time in two days. Alok has a question for us before we disperse and go our separate ways.

'Pawan and Shalinii, we would like to know the famous mystery of HP of our times which was hushed up at that time by our dean. The mystery that brought the two of you together for a lifetime. I hear your lives had been in danger.' I and Vidya shudder at the thought of those days. Raj, Vishal, and Pawan forbear from saying a word. I also cannot open my mouth to say the forbidden.

'We very much want to share the biggest mystery of HP with all of you. The problem is it is a long story. Let us arrange another celebration like this one next year, and we shall talk about the mystery in detail then.'

We have a silent dinner, and we part to go to our own homes, promising to meet soon. I am the happiest woman as I am going back with a loving and doting husband with me whom I am proud of, who is the biggest support of my life. He would be with me in all my endeavours hereafter. I would not have to be lonely and have food alone. No more tears for me.

I wish every woman has a husband like mine.